Ecum  **s**

Political Economy

Ecumenical Reflections on Political Economy

Compiled by Catherine Mulholland

WCC PUBLICATIONS, GENEVA

261.85

Cover design: Edwin Hassink

ISBN 2-8254-0930-8

© 1988 WCC Publications, World Council of Churches, 150 route de Ferney, 1211 Geneva 20, Switzerland

Printed in Switzerland

Table of contents

Preface

Ten years ago an important meeting took place in Zurich, Switzerland, on "Political Economy, Ethics and Theology: Some Contemporary Challenges". It brought together a number of economists, political and social scientists and theologians to reflect on the need to develop a new paradigm regarding political economy.

On the basis of the experience of this meeting, the Commission on the Churches' Participation in Development (CCPD) of the World Council of Churches (WCC) decided to establish an Advisory Group on Economic Matters (AGEM) to advise the WCC and the CCPD on matters related to applied political economy. AGEM consists of a core group of continuing members coming from all regions of the world. This core group is joined by specialists, depending on the topic to be addressed.

As part of the ecumenical movement, AGEM is in the unique position that it can draw from the experiences and insights of people at local levels all over the globe. Therefore, macro analyses can be based on micro realities. In this, the Group goes beyond criticizing existing political economic analyses, policies and institutions and tries to indicate basic criteria and broad guidelines and perspectives for the directions of necessary change.

Although the Group's task is primarily to advise the ecumenical movement, we believe that its work is also important for those who are not directly linked to the churches and who are interested in the ecumenical debate about these issues.

The first meeting of AGEM was held at Oaxtepec, Mexico, in 1979, to prepare a document for UNCTAD V under the title "Some Ecumenical Views on the NIEO Debate". Since then, the group has met six times to address issues like: challenges to values and structures; transnational corporations; world hunger; the international financial system; labour, employment and unemployment; and self-reliant development in Africa.

In the ten years that have passed since the Zurich meeting, important developments have taken place in the international economic environment as well as within national economies. It is important that these developments are continuously scrutinized and assessed.

This book presents a summary of the work that has been done by AGEM over the last ten years and is an attempt to take stock of where we are.

We are grateful to Ms Catherine Mulholland who has compiled this book and to the directors of CCPD who had the vision to establish the Group and stimulated its work. A special word of thanks also goes to Mr Reginald Green who, as rapporteur of AGEM, edited the books on which this text is based.

AGEM is an example of the kind of contribution lay people can make to the church. We hope to continue to be of service to the WCC, the member churches and the ecumenical movement as a whole, stimulating reflection and action in the field of applied political economics as this affects the whole inhabited earth.

JAN P. PRONK
Moderator, AGEM

1. The Church and Economic Matters

Introduction

The title of this book will, for many people, pose two basic questions: Why are the churches concerned with economic matters? What are their credentials for becoming involved in economic issues?

Christians and churches need no justification for their involvement in economic matters. The church has always been concerned with questions of social organization, including the political and economic norms and systems that make up the organization of societies. Nor is this a departure from the gospel message. Believers and followers of Christ were meant to be concerned with such issues as production, distribution of income, division of labour, relations between rich and poor, etc. During the Middle Ages the churches were deeply involved in social and economic matters, not only at a theological level but also practically through monasteries and the creation of orphanages and hospices. The churches of the Reformation persisted in this line and the concept of vocation as God's call to be faithful in each place and in all places implied that through economic activity human beings could glorify God.

The ecumenical movement has always been concerned with economic matters and social and political organization. The Life and Work movement paid much attention to economic problems. The continued concern within the World Council of Churches with such issues led to the world conference on "Christians in the Technical and Social Revolutions of our Time", held in Geneva in 1966, which awakened church constituencies to the development challenge and opened the way for decisions which crystallized in the creation of the Commission on the Churches' Participation in Development (CCPD) in 1970. Another sub-unit of the WCC which is concerned with similar matters is the Sub-unit on Church and Society.

The 1978 Zurich consultation on "Political Economy, Ethics and Theology: Some Contemporary Challenges" was organized jointly by the Commission on the Churches' Participation in Development and the Sub-unit on Church and Society. The aim of the consultation was to give a more articulated intellectual content to the WCC's social vision in the search for a just, participatory and sustainable society. The consultation was a major event in the process of ecumenical reflection on socio-economic matters. It was on the basis of that experience that CCPD decided to create an Advisory Group on Economic Matters (AGEM). The group is composed of economists, sociologists, political scientists and theologians, who try to reflect together from the perspective indicated at Zurich. The purpose of the AGEM is to assist the CCPD, the WCC and its member churches to give serious thought to the economic problems that confront the world today.

The AGEM has met six times so far and its reflections have been published in five volumes. The present book is an attempt to provide a summary of AGEM's work so far. Behind that work is the conviction that economic affairs — while not the whole of human life — are an important part of it and therefore must be of concern to Christians and to churches. The evolution of thinking on the responsible society, on the inter-related requirements of growth, justice and peace for development, and on the just, participatory and sustainable society bears witness to the continued validity of this concern.

Concern and reflection

Concern calls for reflection. If reflection demonstrates significant violations of the principles of justice, participation and sustainability and, in particular, the exclusion, exploitation and oppression of poor people and vulnerable groups, then a radical critique is required of Christians and churches.

To be valid, such a critique must be built both upon Christian values and on an accurate perception of the main issues, problems and dynamics of the systems and institutions that are studied. It should identify and call attention to what, from a Christian viewpoint, is wrong. But it should go further than that. It should also seek to identify both the principles which would provide a foundation for the transformation of the imperfect present, and some of the concrete steps which could contribute to that process.

This is not to say that the churches should seek to develop detailed blueprints for the organization of every aspect of society. They have neither the authority nor the technical competence to do so. What they *do*, or should, have is the ability to identify the main directions of required change, to indicate some of the potentially valid means for achieving at least part of that change, and to test the operations of churches and church-related organizations in the relevant area by the standards they propose for others.

This study will look at the economic order and some major political economic issues through the eyes of the ecumenical movement via the work and the process of reflection of the Advisory Group on Economic Matters. The book is divided into two major parts: the first part presents some general themes, concepts and areas of concern for the ecumenical movement, and the second part treats in greater detail four major issues in political economy with which the AGEM has been particularly concerned.

General themes, concepts and areas of concern for the AGEM

Concern for development

The concern for development is a major strand in AGEM thought. In the ecumenical movement it takes the form of concern for the development of people — their struggle to liberate themselves from foreign domination, their efforts to improve their economic conditions, and their fight against various forms of oppression. This concern has been an integral part of the ecumenical movement from its very inception and became a major focus of attention at the Fourth and Fifth Assemblies of the World Council of Churches (1968 and 1975). It springs from three common convictions in the ecumenical approach to development:
1) the conviction that the development of people is an integral part of the gospel of salvation even when the processes involved are primarily secular;
2) the conviction that the churches have a special responsibility towards the poor and oppressed;
3) the conviction that development must be truly ecumenical in nature, comprehending the whole world and all its diversity.

The problem of the ecumenical movement has been to give concrete meaning to these affirmations within specific contexts and at given times.

Development thought within the World Council of Churches has followed the changing ideas on development in theory and practice. In the 1950s the current views shared by the ecumenical movement held development to be a process whereby the poorer countries needed to "catch up" with the industrialized countries by following the same path to development. It was believed that the basic problem of development was related to the non-availability of material resources and technical knowledge, which were to be transferred from the richer countries to the poorer ones. The ecumenical movement, within such a view of development, assumed the role of a kind of moral conscience of the world, urging the richer Western countries to share their abundance with the poorer and the less fortunate.

In the 1960s and 1970s what was originally a minority view became a major wave as development came to be seen as an inter-related process of social justice, economic growth and self-reliance, with the accent unambiguously on the first of these. The route to development consisted of getting rid of the fetters of injustice embedded in the political and economic institutions within countries and at the international level. This shift in emphasis was accompanied within the ecumenical movement by efforts to get member churches involved in development activities, particularly through action-reflection programmes of people's participation.

There was increasing support for this point of view and the WCC took positive steps at its Fifth Assembly in Nairobi in 1975, where the churches expressed their conviction that the process of development is essentially the struggle of the poor against the structures of domination and oppression, and endorsed the view that the fight for institutional change within countries and in the context of international relations is a major part of the quest for genuine development. This was followed up a few months later when the WCC initiated a process based on the action of the churches at various levels of society, focused on the search for a just, participatory and sustainable society.

The search for a Just, Participatory and Sustainable Society (JPSS)

Much Western understanding of justice comes from the Roman notion of *justitia*, which is basically atomistic and distributive justice whereby each person is given his/her due. But in the Old Testament we see justice more in terms of "righteousness". The prophets challenged the injustices of a society in which the poor went hungry and were exploited by the rich. This idea is built on in the New Testament (see e.g. Luke 1:51-53; 4:18; 5:20-21; 5:24-25; 18:24; James 2:1-7; 4:13-5:6) where justice means the vindication of the poor and the oppressed, and the societal dimensions of justice are reinforced.

The pursuit of justice goes beyond distribution and involves participation in deciding what is produced and how it is produced. Participation is a human right. People should be enabled to reflect on their own problems and to articulate their own perceptions of solutions to such problems. Only if this is done can development be seen as a liberating process, as the creation of conditions for people and societies, particularly those at present oppressed and marginalized, to identify their own needs, mobilize their own resources and shape their own future.

Justice has to do with the production and distribution of the fruits of human efforts and nature's bounty, not only by and among people now existing but also between present and future generations. Justice over time requires sustainability. This concept became central in development discussions in the ecumenical movement in the 1970s. The dimension of sustainability in development had long been neglected at all levels of analysis, but came dramatically to the fore in the aftermath of the oil shocks of these years.

While justice points to the necessity of building societies that will be genuinely participatory, of correcting maldistribution and overcoming the gap between the rich and the poor within and between countries, sustainability points to humanity's dependence upon the earth, and the way in which world society organizes itself for developing natural resources. However, there is a close relation between the two. "A sustainable society which is unjust can hardly be worth sustaining. A just society that is technologically and ecologically unsustainable is self-defeating."

This development is seen as not only a question of economic growth but also of social justice and self-reliance. After the Nairobi Assembly the WCC began to concentrate on JPSS. In the light of the experience of many churches all around the world, the WCC became convinced that participation and sustainability could not exist without justice, and that the struggle for justice demanded a praxis of participation as well as ecological responsibility, and an informed confrontation of structures and powers which threaten the future of humankind.

Critique of the International Economic Order

A view of development which takes social justice as its starting point necessarily views the foundations and progress of economic growth in a different way. In the process of reflection, the WCC, along with many others, began to take a closer look at the international economic order. It quickly became clear that the current economic order was based on persistent injustice most clearly visible in the co-existence of affluence for a few and terrible misery for many. According to the experiences of many churches, it was clear that participation and sustainability could not exist without justice and that justice must be the basis for a new economic order.

The present international economic order is based on a paradigm in economic thought which has its roots in the following assumptions:

1) economic growth must be a prelude to social justice and not vice versa;
2) inequality is needed to produce savings and capital formation;
3) economic growth itself promotes equitable redistribution;
4) rationalization means mechanization;
5) stability and the absence of inflation are to be preferred to the inevitable uncertainties associated with dynamic change;
6) economic development in the developing countries should be modelled on that of the industrialized countries;
7) the development of underdeveloped countries are dependent upon, or even optimally secured by, a continued rapid economic growth in the rich Western countries.

This paradigm of political economy currently prevailing in Western industrialized societies, and influential in many others, can be criticized in three broad respects:

1) it gives insufficient weight to the historical and spatial dimensions;
2) it relies on a reductionist approach;
3) it defines its area of concern too narrowly.

As such, these assumptions could never form the basis for a just, participatory and sustainable society. On the contrary, the AGEM and others suggested that the old international economic order was one of disorder rather than order and had resulted in disappointing rates of growth and employment, failure to come to terms with limited energy sources, growth of a new protectionism and bilateral trade agreements based on "beggar-thy-neighbour" policies, and a global monetary crisis.

Towards a new paradigm

The changing ecumenical concerns in the international development debate led to the quest for a new paradigm in political economy, a new model to interpret reality and to guide actions. At the Zurich consultation in 1978 economists, social thinkers and theologians considered the nature of current economic paradigms and their correlation or lack of correlation within political economic reality, viewed from the perspective of the Christian faith.

The concern of Christians with the causes and consequences of economic crisis is grounded in the conviction that God created, and continues to create, order out of chaos, wholeness and salvation out of inequality and alienation. Since its first Assembly in 1948, the WCC has been struggling with the meaning and implications of this basic theological vision for the way political, economic and social life should be organized. The ecumenical movement is under obligation to judge the economic processes at work in the world in the light of the gospel message. The development paradigms of our world have to be tested by that message and not merely by their own internal criteria.

According to the new paradigm, economics cannot simply be reduced to production and consumption of goods but must be related to people's lives and values. The reorganization of production should open the way to the real participation of people — and especially of poor people, of women and of minority groups — at all levels through a process of planning and the social control of major productive sectors of the economy. It is the people's values that should animate the reconstruction of society, not the goal of private profit for the few. Only if this transformation is attained will it be possible to talk of a real new strategy of development which fosters justice, participation and sustainability by means of a change of actors, motives and values.

The paradigm must be built up to serve the ecumenical movement of the 1980s and 1990s. Its operative understanding will be drawn from the perspective provided by the struggles of the poor and oppressed for a just, participatory and sustainable society and its economy will be based on common social concerns of all peoples of the world. Its policy should enable people to order their total relationships in accordance with their socio-cultural, political and historical biography. Theology should be oriented towards Jesus the Liberator of the oppressed and exploited and the God who has challenged us to collaborate in the establishment of the kingdom of justice and love in which the poor, the oppressed and the exploited will find their rightful place.

Towards a new system of values

A changed system of values is a precondition for change in economic systems. But what values should any economic system manifest, express, help to achieve? During the past twenty years it has become increasingly clear that all economic systems need to be tested in terms of whether and to what extent they put people at the centre of the development process and do so as subjects, not merely as objects, of that process. To understand development processes and the character of international economic relations requires an analysis of the basis of such a value-oriented paradigm. While the ecumenical critique of economics remains fluid, among the values and criteria increasingly accepted for testing existing economic systems, processes and institutions are the following:

1. *Meeting basic human needs:* Does the system realistically promise to meet the fundamental psycho-physical needs of human beings?
2. *Justice and participation:* Are these needs met equitably? Is there reasonable equality of access to the resources of a society?
3. *Sustainability:* Is the economic system ecologically and socially sustainable over generations?
4. *Self-reliance:* Does the economic system enable people to achieve a sense of their own worth, freedom and capacity, rather than being completely vulnerable to the decisions of others?
5. *Universality:* Do the economic system and economic policies focus on the above elements for the global human family, beyond national or regional political boundaries?
6. *Peace:* Does the economic system promote the prospects for peace built upon the foundation of justice?

The values and criteria for testing existing economic systems, processes and institutions are thus based in a concern for human development. This concern in the ecumenical movement has come to be understood in terms of support for the poor and the powerless in their struggle against all systems of exclusion and oppression. That which inhibits their freedom, wellbeing and happiness is by definition a barrier, not a means to human development. Concern for the building of a truly human society — one which is at the same time just, participatory and sustainable — should be central to Christian commitment to and involvement in development. Although this concern is by no means unique to the ecumenical movement, we affirm that it stands at the heart of the biblical understanding of humanity and Christian mission.

2. *The International Economic Order in the 1980s*

Failure of the present world economic order

From the preceding we can have an idea of the kind of questions that the ecumenical movement has been asking about the biblical, theological and ethical adequacy of the economic systems which currently dominate the world. There are pretentious claims and assumptions which need to be demythologized, particularly in light of the results of the present economic order — which can better be described as "international economic disorder". The efforts in the 1950s and 1960s to eradicate poverty were unsuccessful. The first and second development decades failed. The quest for a new international economic order (NIEO) in the 1970s met with negative responses from the rich and powerful nations, and the expectations of the developing nations were frustrated. Inequalities in wealth, welfare and power have increased and an undue portion of the burden of the international crisis has been shifted to the weaker parts of the world population.

The challenge for the 1980s as identified by the AGEM is neither solely material nor simply one of values. Any proposal and any struggle for specific political economic institutional change is ultimately based on, and must be tested against, underlying values. However, such human life values — especially the values of justice, participation and sustainability — must be embodied in structures and institutions as well as articulated in a technically competent manner.

In the 1980s, the WCC has attempted to answer the challenge to churches and Christians by engaging in reflection and critique on a number of major areas of concern in political economy. The areas sketched here are political-economic rather than technical-economic. International structures and negotiations are themselves largely political-economic and these are the arenas in which change can, and must, take place.

Many, if not all, of these areas appeared on the agenda for the negotiations for a New International Economic Order in the 1960s and 1970s but, as a testament to the failure of these negotiations, the problems remain and, if anything, have become more acute during the 1980s. The areas include food, commodities, technology and transnational corporations, finance and money, debt and aid. Each area requires profound structural changes in order to rectify the injustices and disparities which currently characterize them and to work towards the vision of a JPSS. Some of the areas will only be outlined here while others, which have been the focus of deep reflection and critique by the AGEM, will be discussed in chapters three through six.

Structural changes

Why are structural changes necessary? Who benefits from structural changes? The answers to these questions can be best summarized by looking at the present system and who benefits from it, and then looking at the alternatives. Much of the basis of the present system can be found in the assumptions outlined above and in the tenets of neo-classical economics. Major proponents of market-centred economies and societies deny the relevance of justice as a norm for testing economic policy or performance. Their case is that the market mechanism produces the maximum possible volume of goods, distributes them in accordance with demand and affords freedom to the individual.

The normative values of those — including many Christians — who argue that distributive justice is a *fundamental* test of any social or economic system are radically different. They, at least implicitly, deny that economic efficiency can be determined without reference to value-determined ends or that one can evaluate production without reference to its interaction with distribution. From these values flow assertions of basic human rights to employment and participation, to food, education and health, to limits to inequality and to freedom from oppression and exclusion. Necessarily, those values lead to very different institutional, analytical, structural and policy proposals from those of the free market advocates.

The changes which are needed are profound and touch every level from international institutions to the individual at the grassroots level. Any attempt to tackle poverty on a global level requires changes in world economic relationships as well as in the institutional relationships which are a product of the present political economic order. But the changes required go to the root of the present order. Marginal concessions cannot substitute for basic reform, nor can they come to grips with the real issues. On the other hand, neither all radical changes nor all processes of change can be seen as consistent either with participation or with a preference for the poor.

In addition, changes are needed at the grassroots level to allow more people to participate in the decision-making process that affects their lives. This is in line with the idea that true justice goes beyond the notion of distribution and involves people in decisions about what is produced and how it is produced. As people become involved in making decisions in a society, they see the need for structural change at every level, epsecially when questions of development are involved.

The case for structural changes is necessarily a complex one. Such changes cannot usefully be treated in isolation. They must be considered in relation to normative views, to strategic scenarios and to contexts bound by time and place. The struggle for justice — including international economic justice — transcends history, but it can only be waged in history. International structural changes are integrally related to national and regional changes. Change at one level facilitates or even requires changes at other levels. The process and forums of struggle for change are also important because they impose limitations on, and provide opportunities for, achieving specific changes.

To ensure development for the world's poor, two general conditions are necessary: significant changes in the world economic order, alongside far-reaching internal political, economic, social and institutional changes. This means that structural changes must take place in the developing countries, in the industrialized countries, and at the international level and in international institutions.

Structural changes in developing countries

Developing societies should have no doubt about the need for international structural reforms if a just, participatory and sustainable order is to be realized. Their members should understand that the struggle for liberation from the shackles of exploitation and domination has to be waged at all levels — on the national front no less than in the international arena.

The kind of structural changes needed in developing countries include the following:
— control over national natural resources and production;
— effective control over the activities of transnational corporations (TNCs) in order to work towards a process of "selective and gradual delinking" from the international market economy;

— in economic thinking, the goal of general welfare, rather than the aim of higher profits;
— a policy priority for the provision of employment opportunities;
— alterations in structures of power, economic benefits, and institutions which support the system, to erase economic dualism.

New ways of looking at production and development call for:

— a plan of social ownership and participation in production as well as in investment decisions so that priorities are given to production for basic needs and to provide for an autonomous and self-sustainable development;
— the new national development strategy which gives priority to the poor with the goal of meeting basic human needs rather than percentage growth in GNP as the standard against which to judge progress.

All these changes can be summed up in the search for *self-reliant development*, based not on external factors but on internal potentialities to fulfill people's most urgent needs. People should be the primary instruments of development. There is need to place in the hands of the people the means to break down political structures of both external and internal exploitation and control and to bring about the needed changes.

Structural changes in industrialized countries

During the 1970s, the self-assurance of the leaders and peoples of the industrialized nations received several rude jolts, partly as a result of the tension with the third world and partly as a consequence of internal strains within the West itself. These jolts, such as the series of "oil crises", the Vietnam War and slower economic growth, have combined with the challenges coming from the third world and the instability of the international economic and political systems, to oblige the Western nations to question some of the assumptions underlying present political, economic and other ties of their nations with those of the third world.

There has been an eroding of the long-held, highly-valued faith in "progress" and the capacity of science to "solve" problems and a growing awareness that the Western social, economic and political system is not a desirable model even for the Western people themselves. Yet, despite these changes and self-doubts, there have been no widespread positive changes in attitudes among the political and economic leaders of these nations.

The populations and the leadership of industrialized countries must recognize that the growing internal problems within the industrial countries cannot be met by recourse to measures that may have been useful in the past, nor can poverty and marginality in the third world be overcome by integrating parts of developing nations into the Western-dominated international economic system. Nothing less than wide-ranging structural reforms *within* the industrialized countries themselves is needed. These structural changes should include the following:

1) a policy of "energy for my neighbour" whereby developing nations participate in the development of new technologies in energy and resource use;
2) international cooperation on the basis of mutual interests to create means of income adjustment in favour of the weaker nations along the lines of the Western nations' welfare and security systems; and therefore
3) new but reliable and regular political processes and instruments effectively incorporating methods of securing people's participation;
4) finding new ways of assuring work opportunities for all;
5) aid and support or compensation for those most likely to be adversely affected by restructuring in Western countries;
6) a generalized process whereby people can carefully examine objectives and methods of industrial (and agrarian) production in the light of human and humane values; questions should be asked about the social usefulness of the final product and the waste involved in rampant consumerism;
7) the development of a practice of self-reliance and reduction of their dependence on natural resources and food supplies from developing countries in order not to encourage third-world nations to use precious agricultural land for growing industrial or luxury food to be exported to the developed countries.

International structural changes

International structural changes are integrally related to national and regional changes as national and international structures constrain and mould each other. Who benefits from international structural changes depends very much on the nature of national societies and power structures. By the same token the international structural setting in a large measure penetrates and shapes as well as constrains and limits national structures. Change at one level facilitates or even requires changes at other levels.

In 1980 AGEM surveyed the major international intergovernmental forum for dialogue about change, the Tenth Special Session of the UN General Assembly, and assessed the prospects for change as the United

Nations entered the "Third Development Decade" (DD3). They found little ground for optimism and instead remarked on the lack of propitious national and international settings for reaching agreements, the meagre results of the agreed formulations of DD1 and DD2, and the lack of new departures, insights and substance in the preparatory documents for DD3. The analysis pointed to the dichotomy of approaches between the 77 and the Non-Aligned on the one hand and the OECD member states on the other, and feared that the Special Session would be a dialogue of the deaf.

This critique of the international forum for dialogue highlights the problems in achieving profound structural changes at all levels. Meetings of the major actors involved in the development dialogue can only be meaningful if, at the end, they represent more than a paper agreement which bridges in words a gaping chasm in attitudes and intended actions. Targets must be set which can be related to performance and to obligations of specific actors — states, international agencies, TNCs. An essential part of DD3, as much today as in 1980, is a detailed set of targets for action by each UN family organization (including the World Bank and the International Monetary Fund) over the next decade and a mechanism for annual reporting on results to the General Assembly. Included in such targets should be substantive negotiations on structural changes.

But one major meeting at the international level cannot "achieve development". It is important to underline the necessity for a series of meetings, dialogue and actions at the international level which build on their predecessors. This must be accompanied by the same at other levels, regional and national, so that development is set in the context of sustained exploration, dialogue and struggle for justice and participation.

Priority areas for change

In addition to identifying the levels and types of changes that are necessary for a new international economic order, there were also a number of specific issues which appeared on the NIEO agenda for discussion. The AGEM reflected on a number of these issue areas and published some of the conclusions in a first booklet: *Ecumenism and a New World Order: the Failure of the 1970s and the Challenges of the 1980s* (1980). Because the problems identified by the AGEM remain no less acute today than in the late 1970s, it is useful to review some of the major issue areas which remain sources of vulnerability and blocks to development for third-world countries.

Production: Because production is a necessary condition for and a central means of meeting needs as well as a basic component in the power to participate, changes in global production structures are central to any equitable, participatory, sustainable and human-oriented new international economic order. While efficiency is crucial, it must be determined with respect to goals. No change can be seen to represent an increase in efficiency unless questions like what, how, and for whom are addressed. Greater diversity, that is, balance of production and of use, as well as greater opportunity to make use of special human and natural resources through specialization, is needed. Both the balance and the specialization structures will need to be quite different from the existing ones, and will not be based on simplistic lines of labour-intensive/capital-intensive specialization and exchange as promulgated in recent years. Collective self-reliance at various levels can contribute towards reconciling structures of balance and specialization.

Commodities: The problem of commodities for the developing countries is that many, if not most, developing countries depend heavily on the production and export of raw materials which often have the following results:
— low export prices (especially when compared with manufactured goods);
— wide fluctuations in export prices;
— relatively small value-added in the productive process;
— demand increases for many commodities only with population growth;
— many developing countries are meeting increasing competition from synthetic substitutes.

The steps so far taken to reduce the developing countries' vulnerability to these problems seem to be modest. Some proposals have been made since the 1940s and have resulted in a few commodity agreements being reached. Since 1973 developing countries have been increasingly insistent in their demand for an Integrated Programme for Commodities (IPC) and some progress has been made in this direction. The Common Fund proposed to finance the programme will probably come into operation in 1988-89 but the outcome will be very modest. Over 1980-87 the commodity situation and outlook has deteriorated radically.

Manufactures: Trade in manufactured goods is necessary for developing countries because of the inherent need of industrialization in the process of economic development. Industrialization is integral to targets with respect to employment, food consumption and general welfare. It is also necessary because of the relationship between industrialization and the prospects of agricultural and other sectors of the economy.

But little progress has been made towards structural changes. Goals were set at the 1975 Lima UNIDO (United Nations Industrial Development Organization) conference to attain a share of 25 percent for the third-world countries in global manufacturing production by the year 2000, but instead of the realization of those goals we have seen the rise of a new protectionism in the industrialized countries which threatens the little progress which has been made.

Structural changes such as the following must be seriously considered: (1) national development frameworks must be concerned with the poor, workers and farmers, and not dominated by national elites and TNCs concerned with surplus maximization; (2) a restructuring of manufacturing will require all economies to restructure employment; (3) freer trade for freer access to first- and second-world economies is necessary but not sufficient for a long-term solution to the problem of restructuring world production and trade in manufactured goods; the long-term goal is international trade managed for the benefit of all.

Aid (concessional resource transfers): Some of the problems of aid are:
— aid is inadequate in amount;
— aid is inadequate in quality — much of it being little more than export promotion credits; little is available as programme support grants for nationally determined development priorities;
— many aid allocations divert national development away from social justice and meeting basic human needs;
— aid transfers remain unilateral and often arbitrary rather than automatic and predictable.

Aid should not be seen as a permanent feature of a restructuring of the world economic order but rather as a transitional necessity until the inequalities of the old order have been lessened. Similarly, aid should not be seen as an act of charity but as mutual self-interest or solidarity, rather like unemployment or disability compensation. Because aid is at best a support for transition to an NIEO and at worst a palliative suppressing symptoms without treating structural causes, it is self-defeating to seek to make aid the main route to development, NIEO, or social justice. However, especially for very poor economies whose states are committed to social justice, aid is critical. Its presence will not bring about just, participatory and sustainable societies, but its absence or inadequacy can set back the struggle for their attainment.

Energy: A decade and a half after the first oil shock of the 1970s, it is clear that structural changes in our attitude to as well as exploitation and use of energy sources will form a vital part of our ability to work towards development and societies that are just, participatory and, above all, sustainable. This is not solely, nor even primarily, a question of oil prices. For example, for millions of poor households — and especially of poor women — it is a question of access to wood fuel and of access on terms which neither pauperize the household nor threaten ecological sustainability.

The AGEM has identified three elements of structural change which are both urgent and practicable:

1) enhanced globally supported exploration, growth and development of energy sources in third-world countries;
2) increased access of petroleum exporters to knowledge and gathering of inputs to transform their petroleum earnings into broader, long-term development at home, cooperation in the development of other third-world countries, and convertability into interim financial assets whose value will not be eroded by inflation and instability;
3) research for the creation and funding for implementation of new knowledge on conservation, additional energy sources, and improvement of safety and pollution records of, for example, coal and nuclear power.

3. Technology, TNCs and Human Development

Introduction

For the ten years that it has been in existence, the AGEM has attempted to remain faithful to the original directives of the Zurich consultation of 1978, while at the same time trying to meet the new challenges. Development theory and practice have themselves continued to evolve and change. The WCC has kept abreast of these changes and many of them have been incorporated into the reflection process of the AGEM. The next four chapters will give a synthesis and resumé of four major areas which have occupied the attention of the AGEM, presenting the thinking on each of these areas and highlighting any development or evolutions in thought which have come about in the process of reflection. The thoughts represented in the different studies published on each of the areas — technology, TNCs and human development; world hunger; the international financial system; and labour, employment and unemployment — are by no means complete, but they are meant to guide Christian people in possible steps towards a more just, participatory and sustainable society.

Why did the AGEM choose to focus a consultation on the interaction of technology, transnational corporations and human development? The answer lies in the contradiction which modern technology represents, which can be summed up in the paradox of plenty and poverty. On the basis of scientific and technological accomplishments, we now find ourselves capable for the first time of meeting the basic material needs of all human beings and of doing so in ways which would develop the creative powers and potential of both individuals and societies. At the same time the advance of scientific technology does not always serve the common interests of humanity. Often the results of its growth are ambiguous. The paradox is that, while the potential for fulfilling human needs has grown at a phenomenal rate, we are face to face with a world of incredible human want, with the number of people without meaningful work or access to adequate food, shelter, health care or education larger than ever before.

The AGEM addressed these questions in Rome in October 1980. It analyzed the role of TNCs in the internationalization of trade, finance and the production, creation and marketing of different types of technology. It also examined the values and logic which underlie the investment decisions and technological choices in the framework of the world market system and discussed whether or not that logic can lead to the creation of a new world order based on the values of justice, participation and sustainability. The concepts which are developed in the study on technology and transnational corporations are those of human development and participation.

Concepts and contexts

What is technology? Technology embraces three inter-related elements: tools and machines, knowledge and skills, institutions and values. On the concrete level tools, machines and equipment are used to produce goods and services. This answers the question *with what* to transform nature. On a more abstract level there is the materialization of knowledge which answers the question *how* to transform nature. Finally, there is the level of operational concepts which answers the questions of *for what, for whose benefit and within what limits* to transform reality. This level requires a value framework for technology and is the result of the historical and contextual processes of the society to which it belongs and therefore cannot be understood in the abstract outside its objective corelatives of time, place, society, economic power, distribution and conflict.

It is important to point out that the kind of technology we are talking about, the kind of technology that dominates our world today, has its philosophic origins in European rationalist thought. This philosophy is based on the conception of human progress as consisting of an unlimited and unrestrained endeavour to transform nature and to accumulate material goods. It assumes that individual happiness will inevitably result from general advances in material wealth, and that economic growth is equivalent to progress. Among other characteristics of this philosophy are its emphasis on autocratic and hierarchical rather than participatory forms of behaviour and its ethnocentrism in supposing that Europeans, or the creators of technology, are more rational than others.

This philosophic basis of the secular faith in technology and the — potentially contradictory — concept that technology can only be understood within its historical and social contexts do not lend weight to the contention that technology is neutral or, more precisely, that the selection and use of technology can be neutral. The intensive use of the three leading factors of capitalist production — capital, knowledge and organization — tends to concentrate on key decisions regulating the creation, choice, distribution and the price of technology and removes them from public accountability. Seen from this perspective the neutrality of technology is a myth. Rather, there is a struggle over which technology to develop and to use which involves questions of who controls power, how vertical the productive system and its organization should be, what countries and what social sectors should produce and consume what products and what services, and who should be in the centre and who on the periphery.

The dynamics of technology
No two settings are identical, but certain elements exist in each setting which inform and shape the meaning and dynamics of technology in that context. Two of the most important of these elements are power and participation.

Much of the element of power in technology comes from its underlying logic. The choice of technologies to be developed and of the manner in which they will be utilized has historically been rooted in the logic of the holders of power, the logic of the centralization of wealth, power and knowledge, and not in the logic of the majority which is that of basic human needs, of participation and of countervailing power or changes in existing power relationships.

Who are the chief actors to determine who participates in the formation and use of technology? They are transnational corporations, governments in industrialized capitalist countries, governments and state enterprises of the socialist industrialized economies, and universities and scientific societies. The lesser actors are governments in the South and trade unions and agricultural workers' organizations in the North and South. But the majority of the people affected by technology, especially the poorest, are excluded from any significant say in the determination of production goals and objectives or how they are achieved.

In addition to power and participation there are other common elements that play an important role in the dynamics of technology such as:
— access to information and accountability, which is closely linked to questions of participation;

— scale of production and efficiency, which determines the types of technology that are produced and used;
— the ideology of development which, like the underlying logic of technology, has a major influence on the direction and force of technological change;
— nationalism which, as a force, can foster or retard technological change within countries and across frontiers.

All these elements are important in understanding twentieth-century science and technology, for today's technology cannot be understood outside its historical context. It is not something unique or without roots. However, it is quantitatively and qualitatively different in the following ways:

1) the pace of technological change has accelerated;
2) European domination linked to increased change has affected more people in more areas and more societies;
3) the links between knowledge generation, application and utilization for social and political ends by both TNCs and states have changed qualitatively and quantitatively;
4) technological achievements and communication advances have led to the integration in the hands of single TNCs of the entire production process from raw materials to final product;
5) the increased scope and spread of technological change has often created widening inequalities in power, status and income between and within nations.

These differences must be clearly understood as we seek to maximize the positive effects and minimize the negative effects of today's technology.

Promises and problems

Technology in the twentieth century has transformed the way we live. The last forty years have seen dramatic technological changes in key sectors. In food production new seeds, chemicals and machinery-intensive agricultural techniques and processing developments have led to significant increases in output. The revolution in telecommunications, electronics and transportation has made distances smaller, brought all countries into one economic network, and led the way for the present technological revolution of computerization and robotization.

But technological innovations are also full of problems. Some of the promises are in the areas of labour-saving, comfort, and protection from the environment which make our life easier. Technology also liberates us from the power of custom and tradition and makes possible the production of unprecedented quantities of goods and services. However, the use of capital and input-intensive agricultural technology requires increasing amounts of energy to obtain constant or decreasing output. The environmental problems both of goods and of waste and the problems of unconstrained use of limited natural resources need to be faced and acted upon. On the employment front technology is problematic because it places jobs at risk, particularly in the short term before adjustment occurs. In addition there is an increasing polarization between skilled and unskilled jobs, decision-making is becoming more centralized, transnational control is growing, and the forms of dominance and unequal exchange, if different from five hundred years ago, tend to retain the same substance.

In its effects on the third world, technology can also be said to present both promises and problems. It opens up new possibilities for achieving democracy through education and communications, but the power to educate can be perverted into the power to indoctrinate and to repress.

Development from the sixteenth to mid-twentieth century brought material prosperity to many people in metropolitan countries and to minorities within the underdeveloped countries of the periphery. This same duality of effects will almost certainly characterize the technical revolution of the late twentieth century for the third world unless conscious action is taken to prevent such an outcome.

Transnational corporations

The role of big corporations has been on the agenda of the ecumenical movement since the early part of this century. It was, however, the WCC Assembly in Nairobi, 1975, that recommended that a special study — and action programme — be initiated on this matter. This programme lasted from 1976 to 1982. The purpose was to motivate churches and the ecumenical movement to seek a better understanding of the role of TNCs, and to explore this issue from a perspective of solidarity with the victims of TNC operations.

Although the issue of TNCs is by no means new, the post-second world war period brought about a spectacular growth of foreign investments, an acceleration of the process of internationalization of capital and labour, and increasing unification and homogenization of the world market. TNCs may vary in size, degree of horizontal or vertical integration, origin and power, but they have two things in common. *Individually* they are centres of decision-making — and therefore of power — that control productive processes in more than one country. *Collectively* they have become the main agent of transnationalization of production, finance, trade and information, as well as an important channel for the expansion of an economic ideology which emphasizes "freedom of choice".

Underlying their activities is the belief that growth is equivalent to progress and that accumulation of material wealth is the key to human happiness and fulfilment. Development is reduced to economic growth as a linear process.

TNCs manifest an optimistic view according to which almost all problems of society, and certainly of the so-called developing countries, can be solved by the transfer of capital and technology, and the expansion of international trade.

In industrialized countries, large private corporations have gained considerable influence over governments and in the South accelerated transnationalization would have been impossible without the cooperation of local ruling groups which often control the politico-military apparatus.

The process of regional consultations implemented by the WCC programme on TNCs has shown that many churches, especially those in the South, have a more realistic view of the processes of change in their countries than the TNCs. This is mainly due to the fact that they try to relate to the poor and the vulnerable people in society who suffer enormously from the effects of economic, social and political systems and changes. They have indicated that trade very often means dependency, that technology does not always resolve the problem of unemployment, and that large sectors of the world's population are excluded from the market.

It was also pointed out that TNCs, by their own logic, seek to avoid accountability. Although managers of TNCs, as individuals, can be responsible persons, it was clearly stated that:

> From the Christian perspective, the principle of corporate responsibility cannot be reduced to individual morality or accountability. Although accountability should encompass individual corporate officials, its central focus should be the corporation as an institutional entity. [1]

In pushing for accountability and social responsibility, churches are called to use their moral, social and other powers in a way consistent with their commitment to the poor.

However, many Christians, especially in the South, argue that more accountability or setting constraints on TNC activities is not enough to overcome structures of oppression. They suggest that the market system (its logic, values and institutions) must be called into question. They assert that, in the light of the vision of a just, participatory and sustainable society, the market system should be transformed if a holistic human society is to emerge.

One of the lessons of the WCC programme on TNCs is therefore that TNCs must be analyzed and addressed in the context of the world market system as a whole.

If it is true that Jesus did not teach economic theories, it is undeniable that through his life and words he gave clear indications about how human beings should deal with one another: with love (Luke 10:25-37), with generosity (Luke 18:18-34), with honesty (Luke 19:1-10), and with a deeply-rooted sense of justice (Luke 6:20-26).

Proclaiming Jesus as Lord excludes the acceptance of idols such as mammon and false security, dominance of unlimited growth, irresponsible accumulation and profit-making based on injustice and the violation of other people's rights.

The TNC programme led to several recommendations to the churches:
— they are called upon to analyze and review their relations with TNCs;
— they should seek to see TNCs as they are, not as what they present themselves as being, nor as the source of all social and economic evil;
— they should meet with, listen to, and give support to those oppressed by TNCs;
— they must not forget their pastoral ministry regarding the victims of TNC actions as well as those working in TNCs as executives. [2]

The AGEM's concern with the activities and impact of TNCs goes back to its first meeting in Oaxtepec where TNCs were identified as the dominant institutional form of capitalism today.

> They account for about one-third of the output and half the international trade of industrial capitalist and third world countries and have increasing links with socialist industrial economies. They are massively present — especially in knowledge, finance, manufacturing and commerce — in the structures of production and distribution in first and third world states.

Furthermore, the AGEM pointed out that:

> The growth of oligopolistic power and the increase in the profits of TNCs in the 1970s seem to have a positive correlation with the growing difficulties with which nations and peoples are confronted. The prosperity TNCs have created in these critical years sharply contrasts with the increasing poverty and unemployment not only in the peripheral countries where they operate but also

in their own countries of origin. In general, global corporations have tended to aggravate, not to solve, the world's greatest problems.

The extent of TNCs' potential influence is enormous for it was estimated that in the mid-1970s TNCs accounted for 15 percent of total world output, with socialist countries included. If socialist countries are not included the total rises to 20 percent. It is also estimated that if the current trend continues, it could lead to the emergence of a system whereby 300-400 TNCs control 60-70 percent of the world's industrial output, with the concentration in transport, communications, energy, finance and international marketing probably even higher.

In order to understand the logic and functioning of a TNC we must understand the elements essential to its structure. In *Transnational Corporations, Technology and Human Development*, the AGEM identified the following essential elements of a TNC:

— a horizontal network of linkages between sub-sectors of production (rather than specializing in just one product);
— a vertical network of linkages between the various stages of production, exchange, marketing, distribution and consumption within the individual subsectors;
— a network of input linkages with complementary sectors: easy access to — or control of — finance, technology, raw materials, information, etc.;
— a network of output linkages with complementary sectors: commercial advertizing, education, etc.;
— possibilities of manipulating demand for their output;
— decision-making on a level higher than that of the individual nation-state;
— and last but not least sheer size, usually absolutely but certainly relative to other actors.

Another integral element in the functioning of a TNC, indeed its raison d'être, is transnationalization. Transnationalization has extended the horizon of profit maximization beyond national borders. TNCs maximize growth and profit on a global scale. They go where the costs of production are lowest and the expected gains highest. This has caused profound disruptions in industrialized as well as in less-developed countries. The fact that TNCs can shift investments and technology according to the logic of their global interests may prove harmful to the level of employment and the balance of payments of the countries of origin. And the fact that they benefit from the low costs of labour means that they can also benefit from the political and economic vulnerability of third-world countries.

Perhaps the most disturbing result of the TNC structure is that their magnitude and mobility, their oligopolistic control over scientific knowledge, their ability to manipulate prices and to avoid or overcome national restrictive legislation, are all factors which limit their public accountability. Mechanisms which would bring TNCs under some sort of public control and make them accountable for their economic operations and the impact of their activities on societies and individuals are sorely lacking even within their "home" base countries and even more in the "host" countries on the periphery of their structures of hierarchical power.

TNCs and technology

The role of TNCs in technology is enormous for, through their control as producers and suppliers of hard, and even more of soft technology, TNCs have set themselves up as the major agents of "modernization of the world". The virtual oligopoly that TNCs have over technology leads to the ability of these firms to have a high degree of control over decisions about what, how, for whom and by whom to produce and over tastes, behaviour, values and even the identity of consumers.

As the controllers and agents of technological change, TNCs also exercise a virtual monopoly over the transfer of technology to the third world. TNCs claim that the aim of technology transfer is to allow the receiving country to cope more efficiently with its development needs. But the reality is somewhat different. TNCs export tangibly and nearly tangibly finished pieces of technology while keeping control over the knowledge and skills which are required to generate, reproduce and maintain them. They do this in two main ways:

1) through contracts, training, and the location of research and development (R&D) units;
2) through a system of patents, trademarks, and licences which prevent the appropriation of technology.

The result is reinforced ties between the periphery and the centre for so-called "helpful" technology.

The impact of TNCs on the third world is a problematic question. On the one hand it is argued that TNCs bring necessary capital, technology and employment to developing countries. On the other hand the following points can be made:

1. Four-fifths of TNC production in third-world countries centres on the production of energy and minerals exported either as concentrates or as raw material. This prevents these countries from making maximum use of indigenous raw material.
2. TNC production in the third world is often concentrated in the production of mass consumer goods for industrial countries and upper income groups and not geared to the basic needs of the poor.
3. The technologies transferred are often ill-suited to the host countries' production, distribution and ecological requirements.
4. The cost of TNC investment is high with a 20-25 percent discounted cash flow expected. Unless new TNC investment is very high, this means that the balance between payments for existing TNC capital and inflow of new capital is negative.
5. The total employment generated is relatively small in relation to the size of the labour force in most developing countries and often also in relation to the amount of capital invested.
6. Many TNC operations in third-world countries are characterized by bad work conditions, coopted unions and lax safety requirements, especially in the so-called free trade zones.

Nor are the qualitative impacts negligible. TNCs have a significant influence on consumer patterns (e.g. bottle-feeding and highly-processed, high-cost food, often of a dubious nutritional character), as well as an important role in reinforcing the position of the elites. In sum, it seems to be true that the third world is reduced to a source of raw materials and cheap labour and market for the products and services engendered by the centre through the activities of TNCs. In this way the developing countries are not so much integrated as penetrated and captured by TNCs. Hardly surprising when one considers that even a moderate sized TNC is economically larger than many underdeveloped economies.

Technology and human development

What is the link between technology and development? It is not useful to ask "can technology bring about development?" and if one receives a positive answer, leave the issue there. For, as has been pointed out, it is necessary to specify the *values* informing the concept of development, the basic institutional context and the particular technology under consideration in an actual society over a specified period of time.

It is true that technology and accumulation of surplus have created possibilities for development that did not exist a century ago. But the logic underlying this technology, the logic of maximum growth and surplus generation, has substantial contradictions with the human development of the majority of people and with their broader and deeper democratic participation in economic decision-taking. The basic questions that must be asked are: What kind of development do we want? Chosen by whom? For whose benefit? These same questions must be asked about technology.

As outlined in chapter one, in the middle of the 1970s the ecumenical movement began to regard development as having to do with economic growth, social justice and self-reliance as an integrally related cluster of ends and of means. Development as a social, cultural, political and economic process demanded that the values upholding social justice, the right of people's participation and the importance of sustainability needed to be emphasized.

These convictions led the WCC at its Assembly in Nairobi (1975) to talk about *human development* aiming at the achievement of a just, participatory and sustainable society. This is the vision with which the Advisory Group on Economic Matters of the WCC/CCPD has been working since its first meeting in 1979.

The elements of justice, participation and sustainability go hand in hand with human development:

— justice, because human development requires a global search for the wellbeing of all people;

— participation, because human development requires belief in the right of all peoples and individuals to have control over their lives and histories, and in their ability to exert that control with autonomy; it also requires the gradual overcoming of all authoritarian structures and relationships — or the sharing of wealth, power and knowledge — *pari passu* with the development of new structures and relationships based on genuine participation of the people in all that concerns their social and personal, material and spiritual life;

— sustainability, because human development requires appropriate integration of the human and natural worlds for the preservation of both; hope for the survival of the human race is contained within our conscious choice to abandon our aggressive attitude to nature and to each other, and to preserve and enhance life in all its forms.

Human development and alternative technologies

Technologies and technological strategies are integrally related to structures and strategies of development. Human development —

oriented to the whole human being and to all human beings, and controlled by the people — requires a technology which serves the purposes of such a development.

The major differences between current development models and technology and a model of human development and alternative technologies are in the logic of the criteria of technology choice and who participates. Human development models have a different logic from standard economic growth and technological modernization models. Their logic is that of the majority's values and needs as articulated through popular organizations into goals, priorities and targets. The basic requirement of human technology for human development is choice: choice by as well as for the poor and powerless. Making these choices and defining technological choice in terms of values is fundamental to achieving human technologies for human development.

But in any strategy of introducing alternative technologies for human development, participation remains the biggest stumbling block. Even if technologies are developed which can respond to the demands of the majority of the world's poor and powerless, putting them into use will remain problematic. This is because the main beneficiaries of the alternative technologies are presently precluded from participation in decision-making at the production level and from being the major beneficiaries of socio-political and political economic structures. In many cases alternative technologies have potential for responding to the real needs of the poor and the powerless. But while the political and social organizational forms consistent with these technological innovations (i.e. broad participation of the poor in political decision-making) run counter to dominant political economic forces and tendencies at the world or national level, the difficulties of actually applying alternative technologies are much more severe than would appear simply from studying technical and institutional alternatives at an intellectual level.

The challenge of human development and alternative technologies is ultimately not a technical one but one rooted in social organization and distribution of power. If technology is to ensure that the needs and rights of all are met, as well as global sustainability, then we must work to ensure that the poorest and most oppressed participate meaningfully in, and indeed direct, the process of decision-making. Only through that process of transforming our structures of social, political and economic organization in favour of systems rooted in the logic of the majority, will it be possible to ensure that technological innovation and choice reflect the needs and values of those who are now poor and powerless.

NOTES

[1] *Transnational Corporations, the Churches and the Ecumenical Movement*, report of the WCC international consultation on TNCs, Bad Boll, FRG, 1981, CCPD/WCC.
[2] *Churches and the Transnational Corporations*, an ecumenical programme, CCPD/WCC, 1983.

4. World Hunger

Why this issue?

For many the answer to that question is perhaps more immediately obvious than for other issues which the AGEM has dealt with. The issue of world hunger has always been a Christian concern since our biblical heritage teaches us that in a just world the fortunate should never sit down to a laden table without first making sure that their less fortunate brothers and sisters have eaten their fill. In recent years global hunger as an acute problem captured the attention of the world in the early 1970s with the famines in Africa and Asia and led to the convening of the World Food Conference in the autumn of 1974. Its importance in academic and policy discussion has not diminished in the slightest and, if anything, has become even greater as we are faced with the spectre of the recent famine situation in much of sub-Saharan Africa.

The concern expressed by both developed and developing countries at the 1974 World Food Conference and many of the resolutions which were adopted at that meeting were backed by the World Council of Church's Fifth Assembly in 1975. As the WCC prepared for the Sixth Assembly in Vancouver in 1983 where the theme was to be "Jesus Christ — the Life of the World", the AGEM felt that it was urgent to discuss how churches and nations could deal in appropriate ways with the complexities of the issue of *food economics*, and the situation of worldwide hunger, a situation so complicated that it demanded more than charity and compassion.

This chapter will present the process of the AGEM's reflection on the problem of world hunger and the concern of the ecumenical movement. The AGEM's reflection and critique involved:
1) an identification of the hungry;
2) an identification of the processes which contribute to their hunger and keep them in a state of constant dearth;

3) an identification of possible actions which could lead to a more just, participatory and sustainable food system.

The particular themes and concepts which are developed in the course of the AGEM's reflection are:

1) food as a basic human right;
2) the necessity of increased participation of the poor and the powerless in order to effect changes in the food system at all levels.

The problem of hunger

Who are the hungry?

Believing that a true understanding of the problem of hunger requires not only concern but deep reflection, the AGEM started its investigation from the perspective of the hungry themselves by identifying who the hungry are and why they are hungry.

The hungry are the poor. The statistics are imprecise, and the number of underfed people in the world and the minimum necessary level of caloric consumption are open to debate. But it is only too clear that thousands die of diseases they would not have had, or which would not have been so serious, had they been better nourished. Thousands of children die (up to 40,000 a day by UNICEF estimates) — some in infancy, some later — partly because they are not given enough food, and hundreds of millions of people in the world are living below any definition of an adequate human diet, in developed and developing countries alike.

Why are they hungry?

Many people see the problem of world hunger, particularly in the third world, as one of production, and the simple solution to the problem is to get people to produce more food to feed themselves. But the problem is infinitely more complex than that and defies simplistic technical and rational solutions. There have been useful innovations such as high-yielding varieties; they led to the so-called "green revolution", but they have not solved and by themselves can never solve the problem of world hunger. Africa in the 1980s is a poignant testimony. The problem is that global food production can meet the needs of the hungry *and* the present consumption levels of the rich if quantitative physical existence of food were the only necessary condition. But on national and local levels, where hunger makes itself felt, food production differs so much that the world as a whole does not have the food self-sufficiency and security that it so desperately needs.

The causes of hunger can be divided roughly into micro and macro causes. The micro causes are those which directly touch the poor and the powerless at local level. These causes stem from social processes which develop through time. The hungry have not appeared out of nowhere just as they will not some day miraculously disappear into the ranks of the well-fed. The micro causes are wide-ranging and often include a combination of the following:

— Inability to produce. A majority of the hungry are rural. Outside Asia a minority have some land and primarily grow food. But most either do not have enough land or enough of other inputs to grow enough to feed their households.

— Inability to purchase. As social systems become monetized, access to food is increasingly determined by the ability to buy food, which is in turn dependent on access to wealth, productive factors and work.

— Food crops/cash crops competition. Because of export of agricultural products as a major source of foreign exchange earnings for many countries, large-scale production of export crops may compete with production of staple food crops.

— Depletion of agricultural base. As land passes into private hands and becomes consolidated for large-scale production, the agricultural base may suffer through erosion, overgrazing, reduced fallows or increased pollution levels from the use of pesticides and chemical fertilizers. But equally poverty and need have just as grim consequences. If the alternative to using the land destructively is to starve now, the poor peasant household cannot put sustainability first.

— Transformation of agrarian structures. With increased concentration of land-holdings and modern technology and production patterns, small-scale peasant production may suffer and the numbers of landless peasants unable to produce their own food may increase.

— Problems with input provision and access to markets. This is a longstanding problem in developing countries and it is often aggravated by inefficient state organizations, urban or rich farmer biases and inadequate infrastructure.

— Crop loss due to shortage and transportation problems, weather, diseases, pest, war, etc.

The macro causes of hunger stem from the institutionalization of hunger. These macro elements are intimately linked with micro causes in that the social processes which lead to the exclusion of people from the use of resources for the satisfaction of their needs is not accidental. People starve because the interests of those holding power do not give priority to the poor having enough to eat. The many are hungry because the few own the land, control trade and determine crucial policies pertaining to the production of food. The poverty of the hungry, therefore, stems from their *powerlessness* and their inability to *participate* in decision-making and influence the policies that ultimately affect them.

The hungry are the powerless but they are also the poor. It is their inadequate entitlements resulting from lack of resources and employment opportunities that expose them to hunger and to chronic malnutrition. The result is that people may go hungry even where food is available in plenty; some sectors of the people in the USA, for example, are as helpless against hunger as are people of many poor countries. In these cases, it is the consumption pattern of the "affluent society", with the high cost of processed foods, which conditions the choices open to the poor. Hunger can be effectively eradicated only with the eradication of mass poverty and unemployment.

Food systems

It is the interaction of these micro and macro causes of hunger which leads to the complexity of the problem of world hunger. But to attempt to understand the entire problem by looking at it from just one aspect would be a serious mistake, and one often committed in the past. This is the reason why the AGEM adopted the *food systems* approach which allows us to look at the whole as a result of its many component parts. Food systems are the chains of institutions and actors, activities and transactions, priorities and policies through which food is produced, harvested, processed, distributed, consumed and wasted. Food systems occur at all levels and each level interacts with the others. Therefore, a systemic understanding of the international economic dimensions which shape food systems is required for a full picture of the dynamics of hunger at the national and local levels.

Some of the critical economic dimensions at the global level which require specific consideration include the following:

— The international economic situation and hunger: The current global economic crisis has an impact on developing economies, export earnings, food production and food availability. When these impacts are negative or are aggravated by demand-restrictionist policies, it is often the poor and hungry who suffer disproportionately (see chapter five for an analysis of the impact of the global economic crisis on developing countries and poor people).

— The industrialization and globalization of agriculture: Transnational corporations are one of the main actors in an emerging global system of control over agricultural production, food processing and distribution. This process has resulted in changes in production and consumption patterns which tend to reduce opportunities for peasants and raise effective food costs for consumers.
— International agricultural trade: Agricultural trade in both food and non-food products has a substantial impact on domestic food production and hunger for many poor countries through the competition between export crops and staple food crops, "dumped" exports from industrialized countries, and dependence on world market supplies of grain rather than self-sufficiency in basic foods.
— Food security: Many factors bear on present world food insecurity from both the supply and demand side. An effective food security system must begin at household and local levels and progress through national and global levels taking into account differences in production and consumption patterns, application of technology, availability of inputs and markets and participation in social structures.
— Food aid: Food aid has global significance, both in respect of meeting crisis needs for food and — more problematically — of increasing, in the medium term, food availability and alternative resources for development.
— Technological change: Technological change affects food production and its organization, peasant incomes and hunger, both negatively and positively. Some of the negative aspects result from the extreme dependence and lack of capacity for technological choice, adaptation and development characterizing most poor countries.

From these critical aspects of food systems we understand that the root of the food problem is to be found not so much in insufficient production, lack of technology, economic inefficiency or inadequacy of relief systems, but in the failings of social and economic organization at all levels to respond to the real needs of the poor and hungry.

Eradicating hunger

Food, life and values

Basic Christian convictions, the reading of the Bible, and the ecumenical vision of a just, participatory and sustainable society coalesce in the affirmation that adequate food is a universal human right. In Geneva in 1980 the WCC Central Committee issued a statement affirming that food is an essential human right and urging member churches

> to set up appropriate machinery to monitor the food policies of both their countries' governments and of intergovernmental organizations, as well as the role of TNCs in agribusiness; to compare their findings, and consider suitable action, either singly or in harmony; and to analyze their own role in promoting or protecting people's rights to food as the most basic of all human physical needs. [1]

If food is a universal human right, then those who are hungry have a claim to that right. The claims of the hungry are not just that they be given food, but that they be given the opportunity to provide *themselves* with food. Except in absolute destitution, the hungry do not appeal for food, but claim for themselves the dignity of work and an identity as valued members of the community. It is no accident that land reform (the power to produce food) is central to the concept of the Jubilee Year, the "acceptable year of the Lord". These claims of the hungry lead us as Christians to examine present-day social political and economic organization which allows, and in many cases encourages, the co-existence of plenty for the few and poverty for the many.

When the political economic organization of the present order does not reflect the will of the people most affected by the political problems, then profound structural changes are needed to put right the wrongs being done in this institutional rubric. The right to food and the fact that many are denied that basic human right call for changes in the structures of the world. It may demand a re-examination of laws, tariffs, and treaties. It will mean a new look at the institutions which have been the principal actors in the production and distribution of food. Changes in these areas are both necessary and possible for economic structures are *not* sacred, and the right to food *is* sacred.

A just, participatory and sustainable food system

What are the marks of a food system which will assure this fundamental human right for all?

A *just* food system ensures adequate nutrition for all. It provides it in ways that respect human dignity and enhance human fulfilment. Justice demands a society in which all have equal opporunity to earn their daily food and equitable access to resources needed for productive human activity. Justice also requires that food not be used as a weapon or for manipulation.

A *participatory* food system requires broad enough involvement — especially by the poor — in the processes of decision-taking, resource allocation, production, pricing and distribution to achieve both adequacy of supply and justice in distribution. If the needs of the poor are to be considered first, then the poor must have the voice, organization and power to take and to influence decisions and to produce and be supplied from the production of others, whether by purchase or through non-requited transfers.

A *sustainable* food system must take seriously the fragility and finite character of the eco-system and the limits to natural resources. It is important to recognize that "the earth is the Lord's and all that is in it", held in stewardship by the present generation for each other and for future generations. This means that we must resolve the conflicting claims between respect for the environment and meeting basic human needs.

Because achieving a just, participatory and sustainable food system will require reallocation of scarce resources, of incomes, of production and of distribution, it is a political and a power question. Structural changes are necessary to achieve a solution to the problem and churches can play an important role in the process. For the problem of hunger is deeper than the well-thought technical and rational policy goals formulated in terms of, for example, increased investments in the agricultural sector, construction of storage facilities or better pricing systems for agricultural products.

Hunger cannot be banished merely through charitable gifts of food. The structural changes we seek must enable and facilitate the hungry in *their* efforts to assure themselves a continuing supply. This means that economic and social systems as well as political structures must allow *all* people the assurance of the right to live and the entitlement to food and the role through which they can help eradicate hunger.

To do this requires participation because solutions to political problems are practicable only if they are seen as having priority, by those with power to influence and control political decisions. As pointed out in identifying who the hungry are and why they are hungry, their poverty and hunger stem from their powerlessness. When people do not participate in the political and the production processes, or are barred from participation, either directly or indirectly, they have no influence on, or say as to which policies are adopted. In the case of policies that affect food production, distribution and consumption this means that policies can be manipulated either willingly or unconsciously so that some have food or access to food while others go hungry. Change requires increased participation by those who currently suffer from lack of food in addition to a general opening up in the political process of choices for the poor and powerless.

Policy recommendations

In order to adopt policies that will lead to change, it is necessary to understand first why present policies are adopted and who supports such policies. Present policies are adopted because they benefit, directly or indirectly, those who participate in policy decisions. The present dynamic of increased production by larger units, increased subordination of agriculture to input provision, processing and marketing has the support of the most powerful global actors. This is because either they clearly benefit directly or because they do not seriously examine the alternatives. If this dynamic is to be modified we need significant changes in priorities, resource allocations, policies and power relations. To achieve such changes requires social mobilization for political change because all power relations are primarily political and economic.

At what level must changes take place? For structural changes to be effective, they must take place at all levels. However, it is at the local level that the hungry suffer most, and therefore changes are most pressingly needed in local and national power relations and dynamics. This must go along with changes in the international setting for we must remember that national food systems exist within the international context and are shaped and constrained by the international economic environment. The AGEM has identified the following major areas in which changes should be made:

At the *national* level:

— greater focus on national food strategies linking more directly consumption needs and objectives with production policies as a basis on which effective actions can be devised;
— priority to rural development and small producers to increase peasant productivity, production and income;
— increased access of small farmers to land, inputs and financing necessary for production; reforms should include land reform where necessary;

— encouragement of peasant organization which is critical to self-reliant initiatives and to building up power to influence the political system;
— balance of food crop/export crop production so that export and industrial crop production vital for export earnings is maintained but does not endanger staple food production needed for the domestic market;
— development of appropriate technologies for local conditions taking into account balance of payments constraints on imported production inputs, fuel, vehicles and machinery as well as social impacts of technology;
— complementary agro-industrial policy to promote agro-industries that produce agricultural inputs, together with basic food processing and distribution industries;
— careful study of foreign investment and activities of TNCs and large national companies in order to identify and control potential distortions in price and resource allocations which may be damaging to peasant production and incomes;
— proper use of food aid and national food aid schemes to enhance their short-term uses and to guard against their being used as tools of political coercion or as a way of building up a commercial market; the long-term solution should always revolve around helping the poor to become self-reliant by increasing either their production of food or their command over earned income from which to buy it.

At the *regional* level:
— regional and sub-regional trade and cooperation agreements to develop ties of exchange and aid among regional food surplus and food deficit countries;
— adoption of regional and sub-regional development strategies, joint activities in research and training, food storage, marketing, distribution, transportation, and monitoring of regional activities of transnational firms and banks in order to build up national and regional self-sufficiency and not external dependency.

At the *international* level:
— continuation and increase in food aid to deal with the immediate problem of feeding those persons and countries who have no immediate prospect of producing or commercially obtaining their own food;
— IMF Compensatory Financing Facility to provide balance of payments financing to countries with crop shortfall or abrupt rises in purchase prices of imported food;

— more financial support for emergency relief and social and economic development programmes such as those of the World Food Programme, the International Fund for Agricultural Development and the Food and Agriculture Organization of the United Nations.

NOTE

[1] *Minutes* of the 32nd meeting of the Central Committee, Geneva, WCC, 1981, p.74.

5. The International Financial System

Why this issue?

The international financial system is in a state of crisis. This may mean different things to different people, according to whether they believe that the crisis refers to the deep and sustained global recession which we have been experiencing or whether they are more alarmed by news reports that many third-world countries are unable to pay their massive debts, and that defaults on such a scale could undermine the stability of the entire system. Whatever the term crisis means to each person, it is clear that the crisis is a general one and touches every corner of the globe, even though some people and communities feel the changes more deeply than others. Because the international financial system — no matter how remote its decision-takers or how abstruse its technical analysis and vocabulary — affects the lives of all human beings and often affects them adversely, especially the poor among them, both individually and nationally, it is of valid concern to Christians. Those who are most vulnerable to the negative effects of the current economic change and crisis are the focus of our concern.

The AGEM explores here whether the values and vision of the dominant economic systems of the world are a reflection of the values and vision leading to a just, participatory and sustainable society and, if not, what alternatives might be preferable. The major concepts introduced in the AGEM's reflection on the international financial system are those of interdependence, dependency and self-reliance.

Reflection on the international financial system

In 1945 economic ministers and financial experts of the Allied Powers of the second world war met to hammer out an institutional framework for international economic stability and growth at Bretton Woods, from which the system they devised took its name. They sought to guard against a repetition of the financial crises such as those of the 1920s and 1930s, low and unstable growth, restrictive international trade practices, competitive devaluations. A major means chosen was to provide bridging finance to give time for non-chaotic adjustment, rehabilitation and development after the war. The major institutions which were created at or arose out of Bretton Woods and their roles are the following:

1) the General Agreement on Trade and Tariffs (GATT), to promote and to manage mutual reduction of tariff barriers to allow world trade to lead to world growth;
2) the International Monetary Fund (IMF), to enforce a system of stable exchange rates and to provide conditional bridging finance to allow orderly adjustment;
3) the International Bank for Reconstruction and Development (World Bank), to provide long-term capital loans to governments initially for rehabilitation and subsequently for redevelopment.

The Bretton Woods system in its original form lasted until 1971 and was marked by relatively sustained and stable growth, historically low rates of unemployment, and the unprecedented growth of world trade. But it was far from being a golden age except by comparison, and by the late 1960s was showing some major weaknesses which eventually led to its demise when dollar/gold convertibility was suspended in 1971.

The period that followed was and still is one of crisis management, inflationary pressures and the spectre of stagnation of growth resulting in the phenomenon of stagflation and the re-emergence of protectionism. The period 1980-85 was characterized by sustained, intensive ad hoc crisis containment and the realization that the fundamental features of the international financial system were endangered by the very instability and unsustainability of the system.

The international financial system at the present time is indeed in deep crisis. The signs are all too obvious: inability of debtor states and enterprises to pay in full or on time; consequential weakness of many major financial institutions; severe cutbacks in government spending; near-record real interest rates; high levels of unemployment and of under-utilized productive capacity as a result of lack of finance for investment and imports, as well as of inadequate personal purchasing power. These signs translate into very harsh realities for many people in both industrialized and developing countries. A large percentage of the world's population has felt the impact of the recent crisis in one way or another and each of these deserves our attention. But the AGEM has made an effort to focus our attention on the countries and peoples *most* affected by the crisis in order to express our concern for and show solidarity with the poorest, the powerless and the vulnerable.

The financial crisis of the third world

Developing countries are most profoundly affected by the present crisis due to the nature of their links with the international financial system. These links — which in theory are presented as a kind of *interdependence* — in practice show themselves to be a heavily *dependent* relationship whereby developing countries seek much-needed capital in international financial markets for their development, and then bear the brunt of economic change and adjustment in the international sphere, as well as the consequences of domestic economic policies in the major industrialized countries.

Capital inflow and growth of production

The case for capital inflow in its simplest form is that developing countries are poor and their domestic savings are low. Domestic savings are needed to invest in infrastructure and in directly productive assets in agriculture and industry. They are also needed to invest in the development of people in order to ensure better educated, better trained and healthier people who will ensure the future development of the country. But because domestic savings in developing countries are often too low to finance investment levels high enough to generate a rate of growth of production in excess of population growth, they need to be augmented by foreign savings. This much-needed foreign capital may come from loans raised from international lending institutions, foreign investment either direct or indirect in the country, or from aid.

In order to try to repay the interest and principal on the loans they contract for development, developing countries rely primarily on the foreign exchange they raise through exports. In most countries of the developing world these exports consist largely of primary products such as coffee, rubber, timber, cotton, cocoa, oil, etc. But at the same time this valuable foreign exchange is being used to purchase the necessary imports for development — intermediate goods the country needs for development or even operating existing capacity such as steel or oil, capital equipment for investment to expand capacity, and things which the country needs but may not be able to produce itself such as food or basic consumer goods. Trying to juggle imports and loans with the exports to pay for it all results in many cases — in virtually all of Latin America, the Caribbean and Africa — in a balance of payments deficit whereby the money being paid out for things exceeds the money coming in and the country finds itself in the middle of a financial crisis.

Causes

So the financial crisis of much of the third world, which has led many of these countries into the debt trap and the acceptance of severely contractionist programmes imposed by the IMF, can in the first instance be traced to the chronic imbalance in their balance of payments. These chronic payment deficits can at a second level be traced to the interaction between three fundamental factors: (1) external causes; (2) internal problems; (3) structural problems.

Many of the external causes stem from the fact that most developing countries are producing and exporting natural resource-based products which have lost their growth dynamic. This means that keeping their balance of payments in line by balancing exports and imports is becoming increasingly difficult due both to volume sluggishness and to price declines. This problem is exacerbated by protectionism in developed markets which puts quotas on imports of the kinds of things developing countries are hoping to export, as well as by rapid technological change creating substitutes for such commodities as cotton, rubber, copper, aluminium and steel.

Another major external cause of the financial crisis in the third world stems from the developed countries' domestic policies. The clearest example is the effect of American monetary policy on the price of other countries' external debt. Many of the developing countries borrowed heavily to finance development in the 1960s and early 1970s when the international financial situation was more stable and interest rates were low. Since that time, and especially since the demise of the Bretton Woods system with its fixed exchange rates, US monetary policy has encouraged high domestic rates of interest which ramify into international capital markets and substantially increase the debt service burden of the third-world debtors. Where countries owe large sums of money, the extra burden caused by even a one percent rise in interest rates can run to hundreds of millions of dollars annually or even to a billion in the cases of Brazil and Mexico. This system protects the banks who lend from suffering the losses that they would have incurred if interest rates moved up under a fixed-rate system. Instead, the risk and the cost of upward rate variations are passed on to the borrowers. Add to the interest rate problem the sudden surge upwards in prices of imports (food 1972, oil 1973-74 and 1979-80, manufactured goods 1974-76) and the result is payments deficits, financial crises and debt.

But external causes cannot completely explain the financial crisis in the third world. In many cases the impact of external causes could be avoided or mitigated if these countries possessed experienced, sophisticated governments which could lead economic activity from declining product areas to new products for which demand is burgeoning. But developing countries are often faced with internal crises which lead to the destruction of existing production (including export sectors), failure to get out of moribund economic activities in time, failure to identify and set up new growth sectors in a timely fashion, weakness in import replacement activities, societal demoralization and foreign exchange crises.

Finally, it is important to point out the internal problems of a structural nature. Perhaps the biggest hurdle developing countries face is that it takes time to set up materials fabrication industries which are necessary for constructing reasonably integrated industrial, power, mining and construction sectors. In addition to the time it takes, it is expensive in terms of finance, foreign exchange and skilled personnel. But all of this structural reorganization is ultimately necessary if the economy is to become effectively industrialized and if it is to develop the real productive flexibility of a dynamic exporter. In general the more integrated and high productivity an economy, the more flexible it is. The closer it is to producing little other than food for self-provisioning and primary products for export, the more rigid is its economic structure and the slower, more costly and problematic becomes adjustment to external shocks or trends — a pattern which is too clearly illustrated by most of low income sub-Saharan Africa.

Critique: What is wrong with the international financial system viewed in the light of Christian values?

In its critique of the problems in the international financial system which have led to the current crisis with its negative impact on the third world, the AGEM focused on the actors in that system, their roles and responsibilities, the political economic models they adopt and the values on which they are based.

Actors in the system — their roles and responsibilities

Decision-making in the international financial system is concentrated in the hands of three sets of actors:

1. Private institutions, especially large transnational banks: Transnational banks, state banks and other credit agencies (both public and private) have responsibilities to their sources of funds and owners for the proper stewardship of their resources and pursuit of their interests. Development is not their primary objective. Indeed it cannot be, because banks are properly accountable to their depositors, lenders and owners as well as to borrowers. But this does not mean that critical questions cannot be asked as to their social responsibility in lending to imprudent and unjust governments, pushing overpriced loans and projects on unwary borrowers, or insisting on repayment terms which cripple the borrower and imperil ultimate recovery of the debt as well as future business.

2. National governments: They play a substantial role in the international financial system if their power to regulate TNC banks has been eroded by the rise of offshore financial markets. The nations with the most decision-making power in the system are the major industrial economy governments, with Saudi Arabia, Kuwait and the largest developing economy governments playing secondary and other developing economy governments peripheral roles. But developing economy governments, while largely unable to have much impact on industrial economy or TNC bank actions, do have some scope in determining their relationship to the system and their vulnerability to shocks. Imprudent borrowing, ineffective use of resources and corruption linked with private capital flight offsetting external public (or private) borrowing are practices which greatly weaken an economy in respect both to its creditors and to its ability to endure shocks.

3. International financial institutions (the IMF and the World Bank): The IMF's responsibilities are not centred on development or on long-term concerns. They are focused on providing interim financial support to overcome external imbalance in order to sustain output and trade in the world economy. But whether the IMF does provide adequate resources on terms compatible with meeting these goals without causing unnecessary loss of output in the economies of borrowing states and placing avoidable burdens on poor people and vulnerable groups is hotly disputed.

The World Bank and bilateral development assistance agencies are primarily concerned with promoting development. At least verbally, the Bank and most bilateral agencies are committed to providing resources in ways suitable to the reduction of absolute poverty and raising the production, incomes and access to public services of poor people. None has unlimited resources and each, therefore, is forced to consider what uses of its funds will be likely to prove effective in furthering development and consistent with raising additional resources to continue its programme in the future. That cluster of concerns has become more pressing since 1979 as resources available have tended to stagnate while potential calls on them have become more urgent and numerous. One result has been an increasing attempt to apply policy conditionality relating not only to the project or programme financed but to the overall economic and development strategy of the recipient.

Political economic models, adjustment and conditionality

The need for many semi-industrialized and developing countries to adjust is not at issue. However prudent a country's strategy and policies before 1979 and however deep its commitment to the poor, the continuation without any changes of that strategy and those policies in the radically changed economic context of the 1980s is very unlikely to meet any reasonable performance tests or to be an effective way of implementing a commitment to the poor, to self-reliance, to basic human needs or to participation. The real choice has been, and is, among political economic development models and, primarily, between endogenously planned and phased adjustment reconciling national goals and commitments with the realities of the international economic financial system as it confronts that country, and sudden, unplanned adjustment imposed by the interaction of inadequate domestic resources, external creditors and international agencies.

Political economic models and adjustment programmes are inextricably linked as the prescription (adjustment programme) is determined by the economic fitness programme (development model) which is espoused. Since 1945 four major models for development have been dominant. These are:

1) export-led growth which depends on the rapid growth of world trade and on potential new exporters achieving competitive prices for their products;
2) import substitution which argues that domestic market-oriented production is more secure, and that some production, even if it is inefficient, is better than leaving resources unemployed;
3) national need orientation which overlaps with the more sophisticated import substitution strategies in emphasizing reduction of dependence on external trade and enhanced national economic integration;
4) basic human needs focused on productive employment (including self-employment) and priority to the satisfaction of basic human needs including basic public services.

In practice, these paradigms are not totally mutually exclusive, but they have influenced the ways in which development, and hence adjustment policies, have been pursued. Each has different implications for the international financial institutions as well as for developing countries. In general, the financial institutions — and in particular the Bank and the Fund — have not been neutral among these paradigms but have usually favoured export-led growth.

This choice of development model has implications for the kind of adjustment prescribed by international financial institutions. The basic differentiation in ways to adjust is between cutting demand and raising supply. The International Monetary Fund often, if not always, imposes policy prescriptions primarily concentrated on demand constraints including the adoption of deflationary measures such as higher rates of interest, more taxes, less government expenditures, and credit ceilings. The prescriptions of the World Bank in its structural adjustment programmes include the adoption of policies leading towards export-oriented industrialization, import liberalization, dismantling of protection for local industries, and opening up the country to private investments. They are, however, basically supply-oriented and usually do stress enhanced food production.

The problem is that these ways of adjusting — and particularly demand contraction — are not likely to be appropriate as a primary means of adjustment for countries whose imbalances arise from sudden falls in command over resources, nor for a world economy whose dominant characteristics are massive under-utilization of capacity and devastating levels of unemployment. These prescriptions as frequently imposed on third-world clients often add up to a serious impairment of their national sovereignty in the sense of selecting and acting on a development strategy seen as consonant with national needs or interests.

Conditionality

In theory a developing country sets the conditions of its adjustment programmes in consultation with those from whom it hopes to secure finance, e.g. the IMF, the World Bank and bilateral sources of finance. In practice there is often a high degree of external coercion on the part of the lending sources who find themselves in a position of almost total power over a petitioner whose bargaining position is very weak.

The criticism of the *IMF stabilization programmes* is that they show considerable rigidity in analysis, selection of targets, instruments of acceptable adjustment and the pace of adjustment required. The result is fairly uniform prescriptions to reduce demand and imports and to increase exports. Adjustment by cutting demand can frequently be achieved faster with less external support but in practice it has many problems including higher human and economic costs, especially for the poor, because this method brings balance of payments under control by reducing total real production and employment and reducing imports.

The positive side of the *World Bank Structural Adjustment Programmes* is that:
1) they are less uniform at one time and over time than the IMF programme;
2) the World Bank is in the development business and has asserted priorities for the poor in respect to absolute poverty reduction and achievement of basic needs.

The negative side includes such features as:
1) rigidity in considering different sets of instruments and ways of adjustment;
2) lack of consideration of the policy implications and requirements resulting from a priority for the poor;
3) adherence to disputed economic ideological perspectives such as a near equation of rapid economic growth with development and a belief that market forces mediated through price signals are highly efficient means to achieve almost all political economic goals under almost all circumstances.

Towards alternative adjustment strategies

Despite rhetoric to the contrary, there is an alternative to cutting demand, as indeed the Bank accepts. Another possibility for adjustment is to raise supply. For most developing countries the foreseeable future is one of growth and development constrained by inadequate foreign exchange. Neither plausible rates of growth of exports, of concessional finance, of commercial borrowing, of foreign investment, nor of all added together are likely to end the limitations placed on capacity utilization and expansion in most poor countries by lack of adequate import capacity. The way forward beyond this paradox is *effective mobilization of domestic resources* to reduce the required levels of imports and for levels, types and uses of foreign borrowing consistent with sustained growth and development.

This necessitates a change in domestic policies whereby the pattern of domestic consumption and production techniques must be made less import-intensive and export earnings must be maximized through self-reliant policies. The technical manner of doing this will include redirecting existing savings out of capital flight abroad, curtailing unproductive investment in speculation and luxury while at the same time providing incentives to saving through institutions which channel resources productively, more access to small investment opportunities for low- and average-income households (especially peasants and artisans) and increased taxation (to finance public services and investment).

An important element in this adjustment experience is the search for greater *self-reliance*. Self-reliant development is based on effective control by people over their country's natural resources and production. Its central productive focus is not response to external demand but identifying and acting on internal potentialities to fulfill people's most urgent needs. This is the only way a country can both avoid being restructured from outside and achieve a responsible — in the sense of just and participatory — development dynamic. Domestic resource mobilization through greater self-reliance should not be interpreted as implying autarchy or as rendering exports unimportant. It is appropriate to import resources which are crucial but are either not domestically available or are available only at a very high cost. Interdependence — especially with countries in the same region at relatively similar levels of development, but also more generally — and self-reliance, not autarchy and isolation, constitute the valid external political economic goals of domestic resource mobilization.

Reform — working for a better future

Values involved in finding the right balance

Ultimately many choices and decisions regarding how to adjust, over what time frame, and with what balance of instruments and targets rest on value judgments. For each choice of policies there are important questions to be asked such as: If demand is to be cut whose command over resources is to be curtailed?... If supply is to be enhanced, supply of what and for whom? A commitment to the poor cannot usually be articulated effectively by opposing adjustment, but only through informed choices in respect to adjustment, especially as to who bears costs and receives benefits. The answers from the point of view of that commitment, which is ultimately one of values and of ideology, do differ from those consistent with commitments to maximize production as an over-riding end in and of itself, to maximize national military capacity or to stabilize and expand the power and perquisites of existing dominant elites.

So how do we incorporate values into and relate the goals of equity, justice and sustainability to the international financial system? In the abstract it is relatively simple. *Equity* posits the transfer of resources from the relatively rich to the relatively poor on terms and conditions which will enable the poor to achieve development. *Justice* requires support for the third-world countries' development efforts and especially for those which both seek to and make progress towards meeting basic human needs. *Sustainability* entails avoiding imposing or maintaining terms and conditions which crush a borrower's or recipient's development efforts, and acting purposefully to avoid or contain international financing crises and to do so with the minimum additional burdens on poor people and poor countries. To state these conditions is to see immediately that the present system is not very efficient in fulfilling any of the three goals.

In order to work towards these goals consistent with our Christian commitment we must work for what the AGEM termed an "international moral and ethical order". Two basic principles are at the core of the search for this order:
1) international responsibility for all the world's people;
2) universality in the approach to finding and funding solutions to the world's financial problems.

This approach will be based on a just socio-economic and political economic order, local, national and international. Prominent among its values are: fulfilment of basic physical and spiritual needs; justice, self-reliance; sustainability; globality; equity for the most vulnerable; and furtherance of peace.

These same principles and values must guide the policies and actions of the institutions in the international financial system. In order to ensure that financial institutions are fulfilling their fundamental role in working towards a more just international order they should ask themselves the following questions:
1. To what extent have they furthered and supported and to what extent imposed and hampered national development efforts?
2. Have their affirmations of concern for helping poor people been backed by substantial resource allocations and to what extent have these been effective?
3. How — in the present context of limited resources and increased demand — can they act more effectively to protect development efforts and poor people in poor countries?
4. Is their present policy advice sound or is it too rigid? Are national programmes considered on their merits or tested by uniform and

restrictive standards as likely in particular cases to deter as to promote development?

5. Have they taken adequate initiatives to raise and deploy resources to protect the poorest countries and people from the adverse global economic environment?

6. Are they adequately open to the concerns, experiences and proposals of resource recipients?

7. Do they in fact encourage nations to pay greater attention to their obligations to poor people by being particularly responsive to programmes and policies designed to raise their incomes, meet their basic needs and reduce their vulnerability to economic shocks, or — as is frequently contended — do their actual policy advice and resource allocation pattern have the opposite effect? What should they do when the national decision-takers of borrowing countries do not give priority to the poor?

Reforms in the international financial system

Based on changes in values informing the international financial system and financial relations among states, as well as changes in the balance of economic power within financial institutions, the AGEM identified five fundamental elements for reform and restructuring of the IMF, the World Bank and national governments:

1. The domination of the international financial institutions by the major industrial economies, and particularly by the USA, needs to be challenged.

2. There should be universality of membership.

3. The operations of international financial institutions should be transformed to reflect a recognition of the intellectual and theoretical mistakes of the past — mistakes which have led to much human suffering without producing corresponding benefits of growth and transformation.

4. International financial assistance to poor countries is provided with "conditionality". The issue is not whether or not there should be "conditionality", but rather that conditions are appropriate and equitable.

5. National governments have a duty to be responsible stewards of their economies, to act in ways consistent with promoting the welfare of their people, to respect human and democratic rights and to conduct their economic affairs in ways which do not — deliberately or otherwise — shift the costs of national policies and

problems to other members of the international community without their prior consent.

Other complementary areas in which reforms are needed

But reforms are not only needed in international financial institutions and national governments. Because many of the problems in the international financial system stem from such related areas as trade and monetary policy, complementary reforms must be considered in the following areas:

1. International trade relations: World trade system reforms are inter-related with and complementary to financial system reforms because trade fluctuations and barriers to expanding exports contribute both to causing external payments and debt crises and to making it harder to escape from them. Reforms shall include:

a) alleviation of the impact of price fluctuations on export earnings as a priority within UNCTAD, the IMF and the EEC;

b) reaffirmation and re-establishment of the principles of non-discrimination, multilateralism and transparency should be within the General Agreement on Trade and Tariffs (GATT);

c) South-South solidarity and cooperation manifested in South-South trade development both within and beyond regional groupings.

2. Availability of long-term loans on reasonable terms: The problem is that financial flows to developing countries have fallen in monetary and even more in real terms. A related problem is that most loans including IMF drawings have been for relatively short periods, often in the unrealistic and unfounded belief that the time span was sufficient. Therefore:

a) development institutions such as the World Bank, the International Development Association (IDA), and the regional development banks and bilateral aid agencies should increase their long-term funding to poor countries;

b) funds should be made available on reasonable terms particularly in relation to interest rates, grace and repayment periods and performance criteria;

c) poor nations should have a substantial degree of autonomy in deciding on the utilization of long-term resources in accordance with their own national priorities and goals.

3. Stabilization of exchange rates and introduction of international reserve currencies additional to the US dollar: Progress towards reducing risks and costs to vulnerable nations requires two parallel types of change:

a) recreating stable (rather than freely floating, volatile) exchange rates;
b) adopting a new set of agreed rules of the game encouraging small, and if necessary frequent, changes of individual exchange rates in response to differential national rates of inflation or alteration in relative strengths of real economic sectors of each country.

4. Reconsideration of processes and structures of decision-taking in international financial forums: By nature neither the technical discussions nor the actual decision-taking can be realized by the general public, but it could take place in a framework accessible to, and in a context of principles laid down by open and democratic processes. On the day-to-day operational level a more democratic voting system involving all members equally can and should be introduced.

6. *Labour, Employment and Unemployment*

Why this issue?

Labour, employment and unemployment are of concern to us as Christians as we believe that production to meet human needs — household, community and national — is important; that the labourer who is the agent of production is worthy of her/his reward; and that employment (or vocation) is an important way of human self-realization and of participation in creation. Therefore the increasing denial of all of these by unemployment and pauperization is a threat to the fullness of life promised in Christ. This concern is integral to the growing importance that churches attach to the world of labour and socio-economic development. It translates into a Christian commitment to full and fully adequate employment and is the basis for the study published by the AGEM on *Labour, Employment and Unemployment* which stresses the importance of ecumenical solidarity, especially with the under- and un-employed of the developing countries. It is recognized that no one alone can solve the crisis and the AGEM hopes to help Christians understand their commitment and the actions that they can take to help ensure employment for all.

This chapter will look at the reflection of the AGEM on this issue under the following:
1) the nature, structure and trends in employment and unemployment;
2) the problem today;
3) policies and laws and how they can help ensure full employment for all.

Employment and unemployment — nature, structure and trends

What are employment and unemployment and what is their extent? It is impossible to be precise as there is no universally accepted definition and national statistics cannot easily be compared or assessed. An additional factor which escapes statisticians is clandestine employment which is growing in industrial countries, and underemployment and employment in the informal sector in developing countries which is equally difficult to measure as it falls outside the normal definitions of "employment".

We must, therefore, look at the issue of employment and unemployment from a different perspective. Rather than drawing conclusions from numbers which by their very nature will be imprecise, we can look at the trends and structures of employment, how these have changed, and the two important characteristics of employment which are adequacy of and access to employment.

The adequacy of employment can be considered from two perspectives — quantitative or material, and qualitative or of intrinsic vocational value. Quantitative adequacy can be defined in terms of whether a household's employment does or does not enable it to afford a socially acceptable material standard of life. Qualitative adequacy includes whether or not the worker can see a value and a source of self-realization and self-respect in the work done and whether that self-respect is shared by others and leads to a status and a basis of participation in the community and civil society, including in the taking of decisions.

The nature of employment has changed substantially over the last twenty years both in quantitative and qualitative adequacy. In the recent past both jobs of above-average adequacy and employment/self-employment of clear quantitative and qualitative inadequacy have risen rapidly. The former is significant in that it suggests that properly managed technological and production changes need not reduce the overall quality of employment. It is, however, the latter phenomenon which is quantitatively larger and of the greatest concern from the perspective of an option for the poor. Employment is less quantitatively available — relative to the number of persons needing it — and often qualitatively poorer today than in 1965. For some this means unemployment, for others part-time or low-paying jobs or less return from farming and other small-scale self-employment. For even more people it means less security.

Access to employment or meaningful self-employment is crucial to human beings:
1) it is the basic route open to achieve survival and self-reliance;
2) achieving household incomes adequate to meet basic consumption needs is for the vast majority of households dependent on access to employment;
3) participation in creation, in making and doing, is in large part via employment: an attempt to separate work from life is a denial of the fullness of either;

4) self-respect, self-definition and dignity in most societies depend to a large, often dominant extent, on what one does;
5) security and power depend on participation in production, that is on earned income.

But effective access to employment requires more than that jobs or meaningful self-employment opportunities exist and that there are people who wish to take them up. Relevant training and inputs for the self-employed are needed and this is often where the unequal nature of access to employment is revealed. In general access to employment has declined sharply over the past twenty years and has become increasingly unequal with poor and newly vulnerable groups, whose old skills and access have been eroded, most severely affected by the rapid changes in production techniques and technology, industrial decline, natural disasters or international production and trade pattern and price shifts.

Access to employment is uneven along many cleavage lines: North/ South, local/migrant, male/female, white/black, organized/unorganized, formal/informal, skilled/unskilled, middle-aged/young-old. Many of the groups who suffer from reduced access to employment such as immigrants, women or minority communities, were welcomed into the labour force when employment demand was high and citizen male workers were in short supply. They are now blamed for unemployment, rising social service costs and levels of unemployment. This blaming of the worst-hit victims by other victims is often encouraged by those employers and politicians whose policies lie at the root of inadequate growth of access to employment and is furthered by such means as tightening immigration legislation and launching drives against social services.

Trends and structures

Globally rates of growth of production have declined fairly generally over the past two decades and almost without exception over 1979-83. At the same time open unemployment, partial employment and materially inadequate employment have risen markedly virtually everywhere except in some of the socialist industrial economies. Recent recoveries are very partial both in degree and extent. Within employment there have been fairly uniform structural shifts away from agricultural and into services. There has also been a shift away from production of goods more generally (e.g. manufacturing, construction), although this is less marked in economies which initially had relatively small industrial sectors.

In capitalist industrial economies, despite existing wealth and modern technology, the largest and most evident aspect of the employment problem is massive rise in unemployment. By 1985 it had climbed to about 8 percent in North America and over 10 percent in Western Europe except Scandinavia, the highest absolute levels ever and in many cases the highest relative to employment in fifty years. Furthermore, average national unemployment rates are deceptive. Regional variations in most countries are at least 2 to 1 while unemployment of minority group members and of youth is rarely under twice that of adult white males. In extreme inner-city cases, both North American and British, black youth, unemployment rates exceed 60 percent.

In many respects socialist industrial economies have shown different trends. Their rates of growth of production and employment have declined over the past two decades. However the open unemployment which has become so characteristic of industrial capitalist economies is virtually unknown in most of them, and the semi-formal and low-income employment or disguised unemployment so typical of poor economies is much less severe. The quality of employment is — especially in poorer socialist industrial economies — not fully adequate and the rate of progress towards adequacy has slackened, but the appalling employment trends of the capitalist industrial, the newly industrializing and the very poor economies have been notably absent in these countries.

In the so-called newly industrializing economies and other developing countries with large export sectors, the employment structure differs from industrial economies in several factors. There are fewer formal (recorded, large employer) sector wage-earners and more informal (including peasant) self-employed and employed. There are also weaker and less inclusive security nets and narrower margins above abject misery and absolute poverty, which means that the human costs of the declining adequacy of employment are greater.

It is important to note that two changes in the position of the developing economies in the international sphere have greatly affected employment in these countries, either directly or indirectly. The first is the worsening terms of trade for some primary products since 1975 and for most since the end of the 1970s. The direct effect on employment is uneven while the indirect effect via reduced export earnings, import capacity and government revenue has been uniformly severe as has been the fall in material adequacy of employment/self-employment in the primary export sectors. The second change concerns the external debt which has mortgaged the export earnings, present employment and the future growth of the majority of poor and middle-income economies.

Global generalizations conceal major regional and national contextual specificities, but one important characteristic of the current employment crisis which crosses all lines is the phenomenon of transnationalization of production and capital. The concentration of production and capital and of control over most adequate — and many less than adequate — jobs has continued to grow. No similar transnationalization has taken place on the side of workers or those in solidarity with them. In sum the forces of capital and those of repression have transnationalized and acted together for their common purposes far more extensively and successfully than those of labour and liberation. The result has been a polarization of employment, in respect to employer patterns and to quality and material rewards and prospects of work, increasing repression, and weakening or destruction of worker self-organization.

Causes

There is little agreement on the precise causes of the post-1969 global recession and unemployment, but the extreme nature of the crisis for workers and employment clearly relates to policy choices which put reducing inflation ahead of protecting jobs, restoring profits and investment before meeting the basic needs of the poor, boosting production before sustaining nutrition, cutting public services before ensuring human health, education and survival. In light of the catastrophic impact on adequacy and access to employment, many have adopted the "blame the victim" approach which says that too high wages or too great laziness or too high social security cause unemployment and it is, therefore, the unemployed and trade unions who are to blame for unemployment. From another perspective it can be said that the workers most affected never had adequate wages and that the highest and most rapidly growing costs have often been salaries and state military spending rather than wages. As for the argument that people are too lazy or receive too many benefit payments, many are in fact too ill fed, too little educated, too sick, or too worn down to work very hard. Of those the International Labour Office says that 30-40 percent of the underemployed or disguised unemployed have no unemployment or other economic security benefits at all.

These myths do not explain the declining adequacy of employment — they are attempts to justify it by blaming and depersonalizing its victims. They are used as ideological instruments to justify demanding sacrifices from the poor and weak (not the rich and powerful), to confuse and demobilize workers and justify repression.

Policies and legislation

Whether employment becomes more accessible and more adequate or the reverse is historically and contextually conditioned. Nonetheless, just as many of the causes of the current crisis can be attributed to policies, so the resolution to the employment problem is largely subject to policy control. Any serious option for the poor and for people requires making fuller and more adequate employment a priority.

The object of employment policy cannot be to prevent change. To have held the technology, employment levels and conditions and remuneration patterns of 1885 constant in industrial economies would hardly have created fuller or more adequate employment than exists in them today. The poor of poor countries neither want nor need the preservation of the status quo. Change is inevitable; the true questions concern which changes are desirable (and for whom), how they can be managed, what time scales or rates of change are consistent with averting serious harm to vulnerable groups and communities and to people whom rapid, unplanned, uncompensated change will render poor and unemployed.

All policies must take account of historical, geographic, socio-political and other contextual realities such as limitations on material, financial and institutional resources. But within general policy parameters significant choices exist between lines and instruments such as restricting expenditure (and what expenditure) and raising taxes and between seeking to maximize fixed capital formation investment and giving at least equal priority to investment (e.g. education, retraining) in, and employment of, human beings.

This room for policy choice indicates that the employment situation is, to a great degree, the result of national policy decisions and priorities, not of inexorable external forces. It also suggests that the continuation of present dominant national political economic priorities and policies is unlikely to result in substantially fuller or more adequate employment in the foreseeable future.

In conjunction with, or as a result of, policies, laws concerning employment adequacy and access are important in several respects:

1) in setting minimum standards of remuneration, working conditions, tenant-landlord relations, access to land and worker rights to self-organization and economic action;
2) the struggle for legislation in itself is usually consciousness-raising;
3) even inadequate and unenforced laws have a certain value for explaining and justifying action and for mobilizing support for their implementation.

The following are reviews of some of the main relevant policy sectors and instruments at global, regional, national and enterprise levels as an input into the process of informing concerned individuals about policies relevant to employment so that they can make themselves more active participants in comprehending, discussing and influencing them.

Policy levels and their importance and potential

Global political economic policies and employment

To speak of global political economic policies is primarily to speak of globally coordinated policies. Policy coordination can take place in various different forums such as the OECD and GATT discussions, IMF and World Bank negotiations as well as within international organizations such as the International Labour Organization (ILO).

The international political economic policy level is important for two main reasons:

1) many policies such as economic expansion are possible only if coordinated action towards them is pursued by all or most countries;
2) international organizations are significant sources of ideas and experience, of technical assistance and in some cases of resource transfers.

Overall economic policy coordination — of a relatively loose nature — is carried out by industrial capitalist economies through the Organization for Economic Cooperation and Development (OECD). While not a major initiator, the OECD is important because a single economy cannot succeed in operating an employment-generating, growth-oriented policy. Greater concern over unemployment and greater attention to economic growth in the OECD is, therefore, important for all countries.

The General Agreement on Tariffs and Trade (GATT) and, to a lesser extent, the United Nations Conference on Trade and Development (UNCTAD), are important as this is where international trade policy is coordinated. Trade policy can have important employment consequences as it is often the vehicle for transporting jobs, instituting rapid economic change, and regulating protectionism with both its positive and negative implications.

One area in which international coordination of economic policy has been far-reaching is the economic stabilization programmes of the IMF and the World Bank. The International Monetary Fund's contractionary (of credit, imports, consumption, jobs and real-income levels) approach to stabilization has been largely negative in its consequences for employment. The IMF should not add employment creation to its array of conditions for making and continuing credit, but its contribution should be to design programmes with maintenance, recovery and expansion of production as a central goal. The World Bank and the Development Assistance Committee of the OECD, which are in the business of providing help for development, must realize their role in providing concessional finance flows to aid in employment generation in poor countries.

The major international institution for coordinating and to a degree monitoring employment and workers' rights policies is the International Labour Organization. The ILO has a unique tripartite governing body formula with each delegation comprising governmental, organized labour and employer members. Its achievements in the 1970s in concentrating government attention on employment and basic needs through the World Employment Programme and for over half a century in building up a body of legally binding conventions on the rights of labour and of workers organizations are significant.

Regional policies and employment

The AGEM looked briefly at three regions and their regional organizations: the OECD, the European Economic Community (EEC), and Southern Africa, in order to identify the main ways in which regional level organizations of employment policies are important.

Within the OECD the post-1979 emphases on reducing inflation, trade deficits and public borrowing have played a significant role in the prolonged recession, weak recovery and growing unemployment. The OECD strategy of mutual member self-reporting, self-examination and coordination of macro and sectoral economic policy with specific attention to employment and wages could be used to reverse this trend.

The EEC also has programme and policy elements directly and indirectly relating to employment and conditions of employment. Its regional coordinating structures could be strengthened and broadened in order to overcome or transcend national differences of interest and achieve a truly regional approach.

Employment policy coordination in Southern Africa has been focused on two specific issues: migrant labour to South Africa and middle- and high-level human development. The former is centred on the Southern African Labour Conference (SALC), and the latter on the Manpower Commission of the Southern African Development Coordination Conference (SADCC). A good deal of studies, dialoguing and projection-making have been done, but much more coordination is needed in such policy areas as general employment and remuneration which still vary widely among SADCC member states. While a regional trade union council exists, it is unclear what its operational or transnational solidarity impact is.

Ways of promoting employment at the national policy level

The national policy level is important because this is the level at which economic policies affecting employment both as to level and to adequacy are made and implemented. The policy instruments and considerations at the national level are contextually defined but there are certain commonalities with respect to policy areas which will influence employment.

The policies which have the greatest impact on the fullness and adequacy of employment within the industrial capitalist economies are fiscal and monetary policies because these influence the levels of aggregate demand, of incomes, of investment and of economic growth (or contraction). At present most countries still place too high a priority on reducing inflation and/or budgetary and trade deficits and too little on restoring and expanding employment.

In the newly industrialized, semi-industrialized and poor economies, many of the same policy instruments and considerations apply as set out in relation to the industrial capitalist countries. But there are a series of additional and contextual issues and policy instruments which require special attention:

1) the first cluster of differences includes that the international economic setting — and global institutions such as the IMF — exert tighter constraints on these economies than on industrial economies, and that poor people in these economies have much lower margins above survival and that the economies have much less ability to adapt production and employment patterns rapidly;

2) another crucial characteristic is the economies' disarticulation with different sectors, regions and communities at very different levels of economic development, ability to adapt, self-organization and capacity to compete effectively for resources;

3) labour is plentiful while adequate jobs and self-employment opportunities are scarce; this has implications for priority policy areas and the kind of technology adopted.

The AGEM has identified several areas in which national policy in both industrialized and developing countries can work to put the emphasis on creating fuller and more fully adequate employment especially through increasing the numbers and adequacy of employment opportunities for poor people. The areas pinpointed by the AGEM concern sectoral and institutional policies such as technology policy, trade policy, wage and price policy as well as direct employment policies. These policy areas are important in that in some cases they act directly upon employment, while in other cases they complement or influence the employment component of other policy areas.

Technology policy: In the area of technology policy and employment on a global level no real coordinated approach exists. Technology policy at the national level is, therefore, important to control the actions of TNCs, and to ensure that technology and technological changes serve the interests of the poor and vulnerable, rather than deepening and entrenching their poverty and vulnerability.

The key questions in relation to technology and levels and adequacy of employment concern transitional costs (i.e. retraining, and providing interim security for those workers negatively affected) and who controls the technology and for what purpose. Employment-generating, quality-raising and life-enhancing technology with positive effects for poor people is possible and can be made economically attractive. Technology which reduces routinization amd monolithic external control of workers is practicable. How much the positive use of technological change increases workers' self-determination depends on the strength and vision of organized labour and on national policies.

Trade policy: Trade policy is important because trade can create employment. But not *all* trade creates employment and the kind of trade which creates employment is not necessarily free trade at all times. Free trade may have negative effects on employment when it is used as a mechanism for transporting jobs and bidding down real wages, or when it causes too rapid economic changes and sudden protectionism. The issues in trade policy therefore concern selectivity and timing. Trade policy affects the make-up of employment and production and where the employment is and for whom. For this reason *some* protection may be a good thing at some times but for protection to be used as a shock-absorbing device it needs to be combined with policies which not merely create new jobs, but create jobs accessible to the workers and communities who would otherwise bear the costs of change.

Direct employment policies: At the national level employment policies including job creation, human security (of which training and retraining are integral parts), working conditions, incomes and labour organization are important in that job creation is often cheaper in the medium term than the budgetary costs of unemployment. Policies which directly affect employment are numerous and varied and include working week, work-sharing, demographic access, training, mobility enhancement policies, and using public funds for socially needed work. None of them offers simple solutions and many of them divide workers, such as the area of demographic access which often seems to pit the old, who still want or need to work, against the young who are struggling to attain their first full-time employment, and minorities who have been worst hit by lessening access to employment. Training and mobility enhancement policies are important in that they assist people in adapting to change and enhancing both current employment or the possibilities of finding more adequate employment.

Employment policy at the workplace: Perhaps the most important level at which national policy has an impact is at the workplace. A priority for fuller and more fully adequate employment cannot be won solely at this level but unless the struggle for it is waged here it is most unlikely (with the possible exception of some socialist economies) to be won nationally. There are at least three reasons for this:

1) many operational decisions are taken at the workplace level;
2) if one is serious in one's commitment to an option for and solidarity with the poor, then actual poor people must take part in decision-making, provision of information, identification of basic needs to be met, and aspirations towards which to strive;
3) struggle for change at the workplace acts as a consciousness-raiser because poor people's consciousness and conceptualization of what their problems and needs are and how to overcome and meet them are based on experience at this level.

In order to make gains in the workplace, linking with a supportive national policy framework is likely to be both essential and complementary to workplace action. Trade union and other labour legislation is important in that its proper purpose in the context of further and more fully adequate employment is to enable workers to organize themselves effectively, to achieve (whether by collective action or legally defined norms) basic rights including decent incomes and working conditions and to participate in decisions directly affecting them. But policies and legislation for their part must be accompanied by implementation at the workplace. Material minimum wage, interest rate ceilings, grower price or working condition policies will remain so many dead letters if employers, money lenders, landlords and merchants can coerce unorganized workers and peasants into accepting far less than their legal rights.

7. Christians and these Issues

Why we must be concerned

Christians and churches should be concerned with the issues treated here because of the basic Christian convictions about values, structures and change. When Christian values as embodied in the concepts of justice, participation and sustainability are applied to actual economic systems, we see that these systems have not resulted in equitably distributed economic and social development, food and employment for all or global peace and harmony. This is often not due to the good or bad will of the actors but results from the inbuilt deficiencies of systems themselves. The churches, therefore, have the task to support those who suffer *and* a duty to judge socio-economic systems and seek viable alternatives. In so doing we are faced with the choice of whether we are co-workers with God or siding with the forces of death. Choosing to be co-workers with God and affirming life leads to an affirmation of human life and therefore to a judgment of socio-economic systems in terms of whether they promote life or death.

If we as Christians accept to join in this process of reflection and critique and see the need for structural changes, then, as followers of Christ and as members of the human family, we are faced with the following challenges:

1) the achievement of concrete progress towards basic human rights and needs;
2) the overcoming of the insecurity, inequality and selfishness inherent in the "free" market mechanism while avoiding centralization and authoritarianism in state or interest group economic management;
3) the attainment of peace with personal security, justice with the elimination of oppression, and of a sustainable relationship with nature.

To meet these challenges requires a vision of the future. The work of AGEM has identified three broad scenarios or visions of the future which sum up the major paths open to us — a continuation and reinforcement of the existing order; organizing for change around long-term complementary self-interest; or the vision of a just, participatory and sustainable society.

The problem with the first two visions is that they lack an explicit set of normative values which are compatible with the gospel message. The first represents an order which is centred not on human beings but on material things and ignores the issue of sustainability. The second is less unjust than the first, but its justice is not the justice of and for the poor first, its participation is hierarchical and elitist and its sustainability, while including principles of sound management, is that of crisis management rather than long-term concern and cooperation.

The third vision starts with the gospel message which leads Christians to a commitment to an equitable society in which every human being has significance and dignity and where none is oppressed. The vision should not be reduced to mean equality of opportunity for all individuals to compete without hindrance, because such equality in practice helps the strong to get ahead while the weak remain oppressed and exploited. Rather, this vision begins with an explicit set of normative values and proceeds from these, to envisage patterns of relationships which best incorporate those values. Then it turns to technical and institutional analyses of ways and means to set and to move towards some initial, though admittedly imperfect and interim targets.

Christians have a duty to work towards the realization of this vision in light of the Christian assumption that

> the human being, both individually and corporately, is capable of both good and evil, and that each generation, as stewards of creation, has a responsibility to God for contributing to the struggle for more justice in society; for naming and struggling against the principalities and powers which in varying institutional manifestations confront every human society.

This assumption puts people first and, because people are, or should be, at the centre of all economic efforts it is the task of the ecumenical community to work for the creation of just, participatory and sustainable societies.

Such efforts can not only help to create the bases so essential for answering the challenges facing us, but can also help to raise the awareness of the Christian community and stimulate the debate over values and concrete action possibilities. This is crucial to enable the churches to move beyond a purely critical stance and towards a more positive involvement in formulating and acting upon alternatives for the benefit of all.

Beyond statements to action

Technology, TNCs and human development — the challenge of technology and Christian values

What can we as Christians do to help further the cause of human development and the search for alternative selection of and control over technologies? Within the ecumenical movement global concern for human development has come to be understood in terms of our support for the poor and the powerless in their struggle against all systems of exclusion and oppression as these inhibit their freedom, wellbeing and happiness and became barriers, not means, to human development. This concern finds its expression in the following goals directly relevant to turning technology to the service of the poor majorities:

1) justice — accepting the basic human needs of people as the priority uses of, and reasons for, developing technology even if this priority conflicts with maximum growth of output, of profit or of professional power and prestige;
2) participation — recognizing that without participation in decision-taking and implementation and in employment by the poor and powerless they will continue to be excluded from justice, and the attainment of real democracy;
3) sustainability — refusing to accept both the present and future costs of growth without regard to environmental and resource constraints and the moral imperatives of Christian stewardship;
4) collective self-reliance — recognizing that human development requires self-realization within communities — family, neighbourhood, workplace, professional, religious, regional, national — and that such realization is possible only through accepting and struggling for their rights to and capacity for meaningful self-reliance in the face of centralizing and repressing tendencies.

But goals require means for attaining them. It is impossible to come up with a blueprint for action but the following are some of the areas in which individuals and church groups can take initiatives.

Churches can set an example for more positive involvement in formulating and acting towards possible alternatives for human development and the generation of popular and participatory technologies by:

— reflecting on and practising alternative behaviours;
— stimulating the search for alternative forms of human development and ways of radically restructuring the existing order;
— supporting specific efforts at local, national and regional levels to put into practice concrete proposals for technological and sociological restructuring;
— developing a fuller realization of the moral and ethical dimension of technology and its uses;
— working for the full democratization of information and knowledge.

The production and application of alternative technologies can be promoted through:
— the international community and third-world governments giving priority to the establishment of R&D centres in developing countries;
— a portion of the external debt owed by the underdeveloped countries could be set aside to help finance such centres.

Scientists, technologists, government officials and TNC managers should accept their responsibility to:
— espouse and act on values and practices which promote human dignity and the rights of peoples and individuals;
— encourage the participation of the poor and powerless in decision-making.

Scientists in particular should realize the global implications of their work and explore the uses and abuses of that work and possible alternative approaches. TNC managers should accept the obligation of TNCs to make recompense to those who are injured or excluded as a result of their decisions. Government officials should ensure that technology and its implications are fully understood by their governments and that its negative impacts are minimized, and accept that they are accountable to those injured or excluded as a result of their decisions.

In their analysis of TNCs, technology and human development, the AGEM emphasized that the systems which give rise to the injustices and inequalities are inherent in the present global political economic order and within the political, social and economic structures of both rich and poor countries. Therefore, these kind of global problems require a concerted global effort for change of which churches can be at once an initiator, sustainer and unifier.

World hunger — Christian action to feed the hungry
As outlined in chapter four of this book and in *World Hunger: a Christian Reappraisal*, access to adequate food is a universal human right

and yet Christians and churches in developing and industrialized countries alike are surrounded with images of hunger and the cries of the hungry. These images are compelling testimony that millions of our fellow beings are being denied a basic right — the right to food. Many of the hungry are members of Christian congregations and their problems are immediate problems of the churches, but we must not forget that most of the hungry are outside the Christian communion but within sight of Christian people. It is the responsibility of Christians to hear the cries and claims of all the hungry and to start a dialogue of understanding which will help the process of change, a dialogue that goes well beyond emergency food aid during "loud" crises and fades away when malnutrition and starvation retreat temporarily to the endemic levels of the underlying "silent" crisis.

The ongoing ecumenical quest for greater clarity as to what God is calling the church to be and do in our time has resulted in the AGEM statement calling for the search for a just, participatory and sustainable food system as a solution to the problem of world hunger. It is clear that the persistence of hunger in a world that produces more than enough food for all is morally intolerable and an outrageous sign of blatant injustice, distorted human participation and unsustainable patterns of behaviour.

In the past the traditional and most widespread response of the church to such a situation has been charity: the haves sharing compassionately with the have-nots. But it has become increasingly clear that sharing food is not enough. Benevolence in itself is good but it often creates regrettable dependencies and allows unjustified paternalism. The hungry have a legitimate claim for the respect of their rights and identity and therefore Christians and churches are challenged by basic evangelical convictions to move from charity to solidarity.

The following are some of the activities that the churches and Christians have engaged in in the past at local, national and international levels, and they suggest some guidelines for activities which should be continued and stepped up in the future.

At the *local* level, many parishes throughout the world have been active in operating and supporting programmes and projects which address the human needs of hungry people. These include the management of emergency feeding programmes, the resettlement and care of refugees and the education and training of persons involved in hunger alleviation. In order to emphasize the positive aspect of these activities churches should:

— distinguish among their various roles in hunger matters, concentrating on what they do best;
— energize their clergy and equip their laity to deal with hunger issues.

At the *national* level, churches and church agencies have made or reaffirmed commitments to programme priority for hunger issues to extend over significant periods of years. They have also participated in the process of governmental policy-making and implementation on hunger issues. Churches can deepen their commitment by:

— looking at the stewardship of their own assets: attention should be paid to how churches with large estates or investable funds can channel them in ways which assist the poor to produce food or to earn incomes adequate to purchase it;
— helping build just, participatory and sustainable food systems by supporting projects which are geared to social utility rather than simply to the maximization of economic returns or even food output.

At the *regional* level, regional councils of churches have incorporated hunger concerns into their periodic assemblies and ongoing work. This process should be continued through:

— engaging in action at the appropriate levels, taking into account the exercise of different roles in different social and political contexts;
— expressing solidarity with the poor at all levels and ensuring that the claims of the hungry continue to be heard and that food and hunger remain on the priority political agenda.

At the *international* level, the WCC has grappled with food issues through the commissioning of several studies, the convening of several conferences, and the ongoing work of various departments in the WCC (CICARWS, CCPD, CMC) and the creation of the Ecumenical Development Cooperative Society (EDCS). The WCC has also increasingly become involved in the work of intergovernmental organizations. This work should be continued and strengthened and should include reflection and action in the following areas:

— affluent life-styles and their impact on the poor and hungry;
— projecting of a vision which affects the climate of public opinion about what needs to be done and the mobilization of political action;
— posing the moral dimensions of food, food systems and food technology issues to scientists, technologists and decision-takers in related fields;
— making fuller use of the international ecumenical network in church action to combat hunger.

The Bible teaches us that food is a sign of God's grace and should not be taken for granted. The daily bread is a gift and not only the result of human effort. This gift is meant for sharing, because sharing food is to witness to God's grace.

The international financial system — working for change

The magnitude of the international financial crisis is such that any resources the ecumenical movement or the churches could possibly mobilize would not, by themselves, play a major role in overcoming or even mitigating it. Further, the nature of the critique presented in chapter five and in the study *The International Financial System: an Ecumenical Critique* shows that changes in systemic goals, institutions and modes of conduct are needed — not merely additional financial transfers within the existing framework. Therefore, the basic action responsibility of Christians, Christian organizations and churches must lie in identifying principles relevant to and the means for transforming or reforming the international financial system. Churches are not of the international financial system's world but they must recognize that they are in it and have a duty to act to change it.

Working for change should be based on the following:
1) communication, consultation and solidarity;
2) listening to, learning from and working with poor people and vulnerable groups affected by economic change;
3) understanding and action at international financial system level should be linked with action to ensure that governments accept and act on their responsibility to the poor.

Starting from these bases, the following guidelines have been put forward by the AGEM to inform Christian action:
— Reflection on the international financial system, the values on which it is based and its impact on poor people and vulnerable groups in the current economic crises. Such study should seek out the experiences, analyses, critiques and calls for action of poor people and vulnerable groups both in a church's own country and in other countries.
— Critique should begin close to home and Christians and churches have the duty to examine their own policies and practices before condemning others. From the foundation of self-criticism and action, a broader critique and programme of action can and should be mounted, reaching out to question and to influence governments, international financial institutions and financial enterprises.

— The first step of the broader critique should ask critical questions and enter into dialogue about the values which now inform financial transactions and their consistency (or otherwise) with moral criteria and the values of the gospel message. A second stage will be the demystification of the international and national financial systems to encourage public understanding, and informed criticism and increased participation by citizens.
— To be effective, action will need to go beyond enunciating general principles to opposing specific present practices and calling for specific as well as general reforms in values, criteria and procedures both in the immediate future and over the longer term.

Finally it is important to note that such action can rarely usefully be seen as short-term and related to one specific issue. Both the time required to mobilize understanding and support to influence decisions, and the basic nature of the changes needed if the present system is to be reformed into one consistent with just, participatory and sustainable development in the interests of and by poor people and vulnerable groups mean that a sustained struggle on numerous issues over many years will be required.

Labour, employment and unemployment

The history of the churches' concern with this issue is a long one. It was indeed the ecumenical movement's entry point into political economic reflection and critique six years ago. In the report of the first "Universal Christian Conference on Life and Work", held in Stockholm in 1925, we find sentences like:

> Labour is not a commodity, but the contribution of persons to the economic process. The church must labour for and forward all measures which are clearly productive of personal value. The test which it should apply to policies and programmes is not that of economic efficiency but of personal welfare.

In 1937 at the world conference on "Church, Community and State" the message was:

> Man cannot live without bread, and man cannot live by bread alone... In the economic sphere the first duty of the church is to insist that economic activities, like every other department of human life, stand under the judgment of Christ... The only forums of employment open to many men and women, or the fact that none are open, prevent them from finding a sense of Christian vocation in their daily life.

From 1975 to 1985, during the height of the economic crisis, the churches continued to express concern about the consequences of unemployment and urged action aimed at alleviating some of the suffering occasioned by unemployment on the grounds of Christian compassion and being "good neighbours". These declarations of concern and calls for remedial action were accompanied by extensive programmes of research and education which looked for the causes of the problem.

But there are still many gaps in the churches' work on labour, employment and unemployment. The churches do not speak explicitly to the need for collaboration with those most directly concerned — labourers/workers and the unemployed. European churches, for their part, have not yet come to the position in which the rights of workers (and the unemployed) take precedence over the rights of capital.

The challenge now for the churches is to go beyond statements in order to identify the consequences of their convictions and to put them into practice. The churches can only criticize other institutions in a credible way if they apply the same standards to their own policies and actions. Therefore churches should look closely at the composition of their staff in terms of race, gender, age, and people with disabilities. In addition churches, as investors, should look at the extent to which their criteria for investments reflect the concern for fuller and more fully adequate employment.

There are many ways in which churches can be and are involved in issues related to labour employment and un(der)employment: through criticizing employment policies, through involvement in policy dialogue, through direct programmatic involvement and through solidarity actions. The churches' task is not an easy one as in many parts of the world churches and workers are alienated from each other. So churches must start by listening to the concerns of workers. Discussions, reflection and action on the issue of labour, employment and unemployment should be promoted at various levels within the churches and ecumenical organizations. Dialogue and consultation with trade unions is indispensable as is support for workers not organized in standard trade unions, or not organized at all.

Given the increased transnationalization of business, transnational links between trade union and workers' organizations at all appropriate levels are of paramount importance for sharing information and planning joint strategies. This linking of labour can be aided by fostering networking between groups in different countries which are working on specific subjects related to the issue of labour and unemployment.

To increase overall access to employment and limit inequality of access against certain groups, the churches should pay specific attention to the constraints that these groups face in trying to get access to the labour market, and the additional requirements needed such as training, land, water, tools, seeds, cheap credit, etc. Women's access to employment merits close attention; it should include examining the amount of unpaid domestic and other work done by women, as well as alternative forms and types of employment that would respond to women's specific needs and increase their access to employment. Generally, churches should revise their theology in such a way as to eliminate the sexist bias which downgrades the role of women.

Finally, it is recommended that churches and the WCC should promote the study of a political economy of work, paying special attention to worker participation in management, cooperatives and worker-owned plants, relative rates of remuneration and the employment efforts of new technology.